T⅃

A Nation Behind 10 Myths

Second, updated edition

The Naked Swiss

A Nation Behind 10 Myths

Clare O'Dea

Bergli Books

Copyright © 2016 and 2018 Bergli Books

Second edition, 2018

an imprint of Schwabe Publishing, Basel, Switzerland

Printed in Germany by CPI

Author photo credit: Elaine Pringle Photography

Images copyright: see page 246

ISBN 978-3-03869-039-9

Bergli Books is the recipient of a structural grant from the Swiss Department of Culture, 2016-2018.

For Thomas

CONTENTS

"No person leaves himself behind in order to look at a painting," Siri Hustvedt writes in *Mysteries of the Rectangle*. Our experience of the artwork depends on who we are, on our character.

The same can be said of our experience of a country. No one arrives as a blank slate. We come with expectations and prejudices, our own norms and preferences. Adapt or resist? Rage or submit?

Because I am independent by nature, integration into Swiss life often felt like a process of compromise for me. What made the process ultimately successful and rewarding was how my life was enriched by positive experiences and relationships. For what is a country but its people? Through my decade as a journalist in Switzerland, I had the opportunity to cast the net wide. I met Swiss people from every corner of society – from the most powerful to the most marginalised, the most brilliant to the bravest. In my non-professional life, as a wife, a mother, a friend, a commuter, a hospital patient, a hairdresser's client and a dog walker, day by day, person by person, I have got to know the real Swiss.

You've heard the clichés. In this book I chose what I found to be the ten most prevalent assumptions about the Swiss. The time has come to separate myth from misunderstanding.

Clare O'Dea
August 2016
Fribourg, Switzerland

CHAPTER 1

The Swiss Are Swiss

When the Swiss are not busy being wonderful, they are busy being awful. By any tangible measure of success, looking at factors like health, wealth or achievement, the Swiss are world leaders. They have the lowest obesity rates in Western Europe and the second-longest average life expectancy in the world, at 85 years for women and 80 for men. The quality of life in the Swiss cities of Zurich, Geneva and Bern is repeatedly ranked among the best worldwide. Smaller towns have the same attributes of clean air, low crime, excellent public transport and good governance. Year after year Switzerland secures a place at or near the top of global surveys in all sorts of categories, from innovation to wellbeing and prosperity, from nurturing talent to looking after the environment. The Swiss have won 25 Nobel Prizes and lead the world in the number of patent applications and scientific publications per capita. Through the International Committee of the Red Cross they have fought the good fight against the savagery of war. Based on financial and property assets, Swiss households have an average fortune of over half a million francs, more than any other nationality. To cap it all, they even came first in the United Nations World Happiness Report.

All this good news has to compete with more negative developments: the country's two largest banks and more than 80 other Swiss banks disgraced and fined in the United States for facilitating tax evasion; the Singapore branch of BSI bank shut down in May 2016 over "serious breaches of money laundering requirements", the first merchant bank to lose its licence in the city-state in more than 30 years; popular votes to ban the construction of minarets and to automatically deport foreign criminals, including Swiss-born offenders; the ongoing FIFA shenanigans; not to mention countless money trails leading from the world's worst kleptocrats and oppressors to the polished marble lobbies of Swiss private banks. The criticism doesn't stop at hard news. Particularly in the English-speaking world, but also among Germans, there is a great appetite for "aren't they strange" cultural commentary stories about the Swiss. As a general rule, any piece that makes the Swiss appear ridiculous or sinister, or both, is welcome. The result is a caricature of the cat-eating, obsessively recycling, robotically-dull and silly rule-making Swiss that has been so carefully constructed over years that it may never be dismantled. It's tough being the rich kid of Europe.

Somewhere behind all this excellence and questionable behaviour is a complex and interesting people, resistant to simple stereotyping. The Swiss are peace-loving but they own more guns than anyone in Europe, bar the Serbians. The Swiss are rich, and yet they have the lowest rate of home-ownership in the industrialised world. They stand accused of xenophobia and being insular but every fourth person living in Switzerland is foreign-born. Swiss women had to wait longer than their European sisters for key rights but they have the highest rate of workforce participation in Europe, and the lowest abortion rate, coupled with relaxed abortion laws. Though the Swiss are neutral, they are involved behind the scenes in numerous international conflicts. The Swiss are boring (the *Financial Times* will tell you "why 'happy' is boring"), but they have a great sex life (if you believe the Durex Sexual Wellbeing Survey).

Stellar rankings in the Global Innovation Index, the Legatum Prosperity Index, the Country Brand Index, the IMD World Talent Report, the Global Competitiveness Index and the Environmental Performance Index, to name but a few, show the bright and shining nation Swiss officialdom wants us to see. The Swiss care what other countries think of them. Since 1970, successive acts of parliament have been introduced to ensure large amounts of time and money are invested in promoting Switzerland's image abroad and supporting "the stimulation of positive feelings towards Switzerland". The Federal Department of Foreign Affairs has a unit dedicated to nation branding abroad, Presence Switzerland (annual budget eight million francs), which implements the government's communication strategy, and organises a strong marketing presence at major international events, such as World Expos or Olympic Games. The brand used for these events is House of Switzerland, which can take different forms. At the Sochi Winter Olympics in 2014, for example, a 730-square-metre transportable wooden guest centre was erected, showcasing Swiss innovation and products. The budget for the Swiss presence in Sochi was three million francs. The Swiss venue in the fan zone at the football World Cup in Rio de Janeiro boasted 240,000 visitors the same year. Evidently the government feels it is getting a good return from these promotional exercises. Some six million francs were earmarked for the 2016 Summer Olympics in Rio where the 4,100-square-metre Swiss space featured three houses and a park.

Thanks to these efforts, plus the largely positive experiences of millions of tourists, students and expats, and the success of the national brand, the Swiss have managed to soften serious reputational blows, such as the scandal about Holocaust-era accounts at the end of the 1990s, a series of openly xenophobic votes, and various banking scandals. Not only that, official

The House of Switzerland made its debut in Sochi

Switzerland manages to successfully project two flattering but contradictory images side-by-side – the rural mountain idyll populated by docile cows and wholesome country folk, on the one hand, and the cutting-edge high-tech hub populated by a brilliant, innovative workforce, on the other hand. This Janus-like representation is so successful that even the Swiss themselves are no longer sure which ideal they reflect. Switzerland has one of the strongest national brands in the world, ranked between fifth and eighth in the Anholt Branding index, and occupying first or second place in the FutureBrand Country Brand Index in recent years. The strength of a country brand is connected to how many well-known consumer brands originate or are produced in the country. Along with Switzerland, countries like Japan, Canada and Germany consistently do well. A *Forbes* magazine report on the Country Brand rankings said of Switzerland: "Consider it the Apple of the world."

Switzerland as a brand is associated with tangible things such as chocolate, the Matterhorn, Heidi, banks, luxury watches, its national railway system and high-end mountain resorts, but also with more abstract qualities such as wealth, unspoilt nature, high tech, direct democracy, pleasure and culture, according to marketing expert Klaus-Dieter Koch.

National clichés take a long time to become established and do not reach critical mass without a significant kernel of truth. But once these images have crystallised, the full picture is obscured and the real people are no longer knowable under all the layers of assumptions. In these pages, I will stress test those clichés by examining the facts and the individuals behind them, and introduce you to a people free from the different costumes they wear, from street sweeper to city banker. But before we look further at the achievements and failings of the Swiss, we need to know who we're talking about. A French artist with Swiss roots, Ben Vautier, had some fun at the Seville Expo in 1992, by choosing the motto *La Suisse n'existe pas* (Switzerland does not exist) for the official Swiss pavilion. He was echoing an idea that had already been part of the debate in French-speaking Switzerland since the 1970s, questioning the place of the French-speaking Swiss *(les Romands)* in the wider French-speaking world and within a majority German-speaking country. Switzerland might not be a homogenous cultural space, but it does have a flag, a parliament, an army and a currency, so I guess we can agree it exists. But do the Swiss exist? And if so, who are they?

We are Switzerland

Honegger is a Swiss facility management and services company. That means it looks after buildings for other companies, taking over tasks like cleaning and maintenance. To celebrate 66 years in business, Honegger ran a national advertising campaign, featuring smiling portraits of its employees, with the

WIR SIND SCHWEIZ

The 2015 campaign featured this group picture and posters of the individual workers

slogan "We Are Switzerland", and in smaller type: "6,000 Workers, More than 100 Nations, One Homeland!"

It was a big-budget campaign. The Honegger faces, of different ethnic backgrounds, were to be seen everywhere – on the sides of buses, in newspapers, on billboards. The company proudly declared it was a traditional family business, known for "Swiss values of reliability, fairness, openness and cleanliness". By showing off its foreign employees, Honegger was expressing confidence that these values could be embodied by an international workforce. Diversity is the order of the day in Switzerland, and not just among the migrant population.

With four national language groups, the Swiss are a multicultural nation, even before recent migration comes into play. Historically, the country's location at the crossroads of Europe surrounded by a hinterland of fellow French-, German- and Italian-speakers produced a lot of moving and mixing over the generations. The Swiss also emigrated in significant numbers to the New World and other far-flung destinations. To go further back into the mists of time, the early settlers of Swiss territory were Celts, the most important tribe being the Helvetians. Their name lives on in the official Latin name of Switzerland – *Confoederatio Helvetica* (hence the country domain .ch). The Celts gave way to the Romans, who in turn ceded to the Germanic tribes.

Today half of Swiss people have at least one foreign grandparent, while one in four of the resident population is foreign. In what sense foreign? There are two, or possibly three, ways of looking at this. By one count foreigners are individuals from other countries who have come to live in Switzerland (some of whom, like me, may have acquired Swiss nationality and speak Swiss languages with an accent). By another definition, anyone living in Switzerland who does not possess Swiss citizenship is foreign (including those who were born and educated in Switzerland, and can pass for Swiss). Both definitions describe roughly one-in-four residents of Switzerland today. A more nativist view, however, says no one is truly Swiss who does not have Swiss blood. This would include the 762,000 Swiss citizens living abroad (first, second, third generation, ad infinitum) but exclude the latter two sets of "foreigners", regardless of identity papers.

Join the club
Whatever way you look at it, the Swiss defy simple categorisation. They are French-speaking, German-speaking, Italian-speaking and Romansh-speaking. The Swiss are Catholic; the Swiss are Protestant. The Swiss have foreign grandparents; the Swiss have foreign parents. The Swiss are people who were born abroad or in Switzerland and became naturalised citizens (8%). The Swiss are Yenish gypsies (a community 30,000-strong that has lived in Switzerland for generations). All this diversity makes any generalisation about the Swiss character difficult or

even pointless, and yet, for better or worse, all of these so-called Swiss have chosen to create together a society that inevitably reflects something about them.

In contrast to other European countries, Switzerland came into being as a gradually expanding jigsaw puzzle, based more on alliances than conquest. The German term for this free-will formula, *Willensnation Schweiz* (nation by volition), is favoured by historians and still pops up in newspaper editorials and political debate. The pieces of the jigsaw are the 26 cantons, and they owe their existence to the Alps, or more precisely the pack mule drivers of the Gotthard Pass, which is reached from the north through the canton of Uri. As the shortest north-south trade route over the Alps, the pass had been in use as a mule track since Roman times but it was a difficult route. It took the building of two bridges in the thirteenth century to attract more travellers, turning it into the most popular Alpine pass of its day, connecting the dynamic regions of Lombardy in the south with the German states, and Champagne and Flanders in the north. The steady trade southwards in cheese, cloth, leather and metal goods crossed paths with cereals, wine, leather, oil, silk, and cotton from warmer climes heading north, a lucrative business for those providing transport and operating the customs posts.

The first three pieces of the jigsaw – Uri, Schwyz and Unterwalden (later split into two parts, Obwalden and Nidwalden) – wanted independence in order to have full control of the pass and their livelihoods, so they made a pact in 1291 to determine their own future, free from interference by the House of Habsburg. The upstarts of the Old Swiss Confederacy became known, disparagingly at first, as the *Schwyzer*, after the canton, and gradually came to refer to themselves by this name. Although it would take another 500 years before the jigsaw would grow into the shape that we know as modern Switzerland, a new

Winterreise 1790 über den Gotthard (Winter journey 1790 over the Gotthard) by the German painter Friedrich Wilhelm Rothe, from a drawing by Johann Gottfried Jentzsch

brand was born, one based on three pillars: trade, solidarity and self-determination.

If the cantons can be described as pieces of a jigsaw puzzle, the people of Switzerland are also a set of unique pieces that fit together. Because of the geographical factors already mentioned and widespread intermarriage with other nationalities, a narrow definition of Swiss leaves us with a small group. Families exclusively made up of native Swiss and their descendants are now a minority in Switzerland. Roger Federer, with his South African-born mother and all his triumphs, is not one hundred per cent Swiss. But nobody would dream of excluding the Swiss with one foreign parent, including my children, from the national family; they are a very welcome and sizeable piece of the puzzle.

But what of the people who are Swiss by choice? These naturalised citizens, myself and Albert Einstein included, are true to the *Willensnation* heritage of Switzerland. Coming from other cultures, we are not typically Swiss but we accept the Swiss project as a worthwhile undertaking and we have adopted a Swiss way of life, whether we realise it or not. We tut-tut when the train is three minutes late, we think it's normal for all members of society to have equal access to the best healthcare and education, and we take a position on important national questions, such as which is the better supermarket chain – Coop or Migros.

But we did not grow up here. Another important piece of the puzzle is represented by those who have had a Swiss childhood and know no other country as intimately as they know Switzerland. Loosely referred to as *Secondos*, two thirds of these 500,000 second generation immigrants do not have Swiss nationality, for a host of reasons. Some are discouraged or even disqualified by the high hurdles to naturalisation, while others may wish to remain loyal to their parents' nationality. This group, with their close understanding of the country and a life of Swiss experiences and Swiss expectations, are Swiss in all but name. Both the *Secondos* and the naturalised Swiss are living proof that you can be Swiss and foreign at the same time.

To whom am I referring in this book when I talk about the Swiss? The answer does not fit neatly with statistical definitions. The Swiss of this book are a combination of Swiss citizens and Swiss residents: essentially people who have absorbed a significant quotient of Swissness into their character. With the exception of popular votes, the statistics and studies I have drawn on to give a picture of Swiss society refer more often to the Swiss population in general than Swiss citizens in particular. My broad definition of Swiss includes people who have been moulded by Switzerland and who contribute to the country, whether negatively or positively. Their identity papers and ethnic origin are not my main concern. In much the same way that we have learnt to understand the importance of gender identity as opposed to biological sex, there is room in my definition of Swiss for anyone who feels Swiss inside.

CHAPTER 2

The Swiss Are Rich

If you can't even say "The Swiss Are Swiss" without a long list of caveats and explanations, things look shaky for some of the other clichés attached to the Swiss. So let's move next to a statement everyone knows to be true: The Swiss are rich.

Right?

Sort of. If the legendary Swiss music star Tina Turner (she renounced her US citizenship in 2013) held a cocktail party at her luxury home overlooking Lake Zurich, and invited 1,000 people who were a perfectly representative cross-section of Swiss households, an astounding 135 of the guests would be millionaires like her.

Switzerland has the highest density of millionaires in the world, defined as people with assets above one million US dollars, not counting the value of their residence or business. The hostess, net worth of $250 million, would be the only person at the party to qualify as an ultra-high net worth individual (with assets of more than $100 million). Switzerland has the fourth-highest density of this category of super rich households in the world, with just under one per 1,000.

We don't have CVs for all of these jet-setters, but *Bilanz* magazine's annual list of Switzerland's richest residents tells us that the super-rich in Switzerland include members of family businesses – dynasties, such as the Bertarelli family (net worth $13 billion), who made their fortune in the biotech sector with fertility drugs; the Hoffmann-Oeri clan (worth $24 billion), who control Roche pharmaceutical company – and plenty of foreign-born magnates, like Russian billionaire Viktor Vekselberg ($13 billion in diverse holdings) and Charlene de Carvalho-Heineken (net worth $12 billion) of the Dutch brewing dynasty.

And the rich are getting richer. The first edition of the *Bilanz* rich list in 1989 featured the top one hundred fortunes, with a combined wealth of 69 billion francs, or four billion francs less than the 73 billion owned by just two families in 2016: Ikea's Kamprad family, and the Brazilian-Swiss billionaire with a finger in every pie, Jorge Lemann.

The Boston Consulting Group reports that Switzerland is not simply a haven for foreign capital. In fact, the amount of money held by Swiss residents in Swiss banks is slightly higher than the money deposited from beyond Swiss borders: $2.5 trillion versus $2.4 trillion in 2016.

Swiss wealth is an undeniable fact. One of the most accurate measures of wealth is gross domestic product (GDP) per capita at purchasing power parity (PPP), which takes into account the cost of living. In 2015 Switzerland's was $58,731, placing the median Swiss at ninth place in the world rankings of personal wealth. The only other European countries ranked higher in this league were Norway and Luxembourg (San Marino too if we're counting microstates). The GDP (PPP) for the United States was not far behind Switzerland at $56,421. Canada, Germany and Australia were in the $45,000 to $47,000 range, while the UK and France produced around $41,000 per capita.

But there's more to wealth than GDP. In the 2016 Credit Suisse wealth report, which calculated individual wealth based on financial assets plus real assets (mainly property) owned by households minus their debts, Swiss residents came out as the richest in the world. Under this calculation, adults in Switzerland have an average fortune of $537,600, head and shoulders above the rest of the top ten, of which only one country, Australia in second place, made it above $400,000. It must be said, however, that a relatively small number of fabulously wealthy people at the top haul the Swiss average upwards. More than one third of Swiss adults have assets below $100,000.

This wealth covers the country like furniture polish, making the roads and rooftops shine. It exists on two levels – in

TOP TEN COUNTRIES WITH THE HIGHEST
AVERAGE WEALTH PER ADULT IN MID-2016

Ranking	Country	Wealth Per Average Wealth Per Adult (in USD)
1	Switzerland	537,600
2	Australia	402,600
3	United States	388,600
4	New Zealand	337,400
5	Norway	320,500
6	Denmark	281,500
7	Belgium	278,100
8	United Kingdom	278,000
9	Singapore	268,800
10	France	263,400

Credit Suisse Global Wealth Report 2016

citizens' pockets and in the public coffers. It is there in the purse of the little old lady who, without batting an eyelid, pays for her five-franc coffee with a hundred-franc note. It is there in the meticulously restored medieval facades and the over-equipped hospitals. Being in possession of such wealth influences policymaking and individual attitudes, sometimes in a divisive way.

When did the Swiss get so rich?
The Swiss have only themselves to thank for their wealth, goes one line of argument. Hard work and initiative was all it took. Not so fast, counter others; Switzerland's wealth can be traced to one infamous factor: banking secrecy.

So which is it? According to comparative figures for disposable income in European countries, compiled annually in euros by the Swiss Federal Statistics Office, the only countries where consumers are better off than the Swiss are Luxembourg and Norway. After paying taxes and living expenses, the average Swiss household these days has more than €25,000 in disposable income for spending and saving annually, well above their neighbours (France and Germany hover under €20,000, in Britain the figure is just under €17,000). But up until the First World War, Swiss workers were worse off than their neighbours in terms of real wages. Although the country was economically successful, there was a delay in workers benefiting from that prosperity. The Swiss catch-up and eventual overtaking of almost every other European economy took place between the First World War and 1950.

Roman Studer at the University of St Gallen challenges the popular explanation that the Swiss work ethic, education level and culture of entrepreneurship alone enabled Switzerland's rise to unexpected heights. For this "Protestant ethic" explanation to stand up, Switzerland would have to have been making steady progress along the road to prosperity for a long time, well before the Industrial Revolution, he argues.

The nineteenth century was a time of great opportunities for the Swiss. As a small open economy specialising in niche exports, Switzerland was able to carve out a lucrative position in the rapidly expanding global market. A significant portion of European prosperity of that era came from colonialism but you didn't have to be a colonial power to make hay, as German economist Arwed Emminghaus pointed out in 1861:

> The small, land-locked country [of Switzerland] had set up a sort of 'colonial system' without possessing a fleet, without maintaining any colonial administration, without having had to wage any wars, and without having been forced to resort to any kind of oppression.

Emminghaus was referring to the Swiss businessmen who had set up trading posts in numerous far-flung places, from Manila to the Gold Coast colony (present day Ghana), positioning themselves in a way that would prove to be highly profitable over the long term. The global trading business, originally dominated by the maritime powers, was opened up when the United Kingdom became a convert to free trade in 1849. The Volkart brothers from Winterthur were among the first to react, opening an office in Bombay in 1851. Initially they imported cotton from India, and later a whole array of tropical products. Two takeovers later, the coffee business is still trading as British-owned Volcafe. But apart from a handful of tenacious companies, like DKSH and Zuellig, most of the old Swiss names are gone. The Swiss-based companies that dominate international commodities trading now, including the trade in crude oil, sugar, copper, zinc and grains, are only recent arrivals on the scene – but are grafted onto a long tradition.

Another "free-rider feature" that worked to Switzerland's benefit was the absence of a patent law until 1907. Successful Swiss companies simply stole intellectual property, as Studer writes:

> Denounced as 'practices of robber barons' and 'a system of parasitism' by foreign competitors, this institutional anomaly is believed to have facilitated the emergence of powerful food-processing, chemical, and engineering industries in the late nineteenth century, as Swiss entrepreneurs could adopt new technologies without having to bear any of the high development costs.

Studer sees today's affluence mainly as a dividend from political stability and neutrality in the twentieth century. Financial institutions are the cornerstone of this analysis but there was much more than just banking secrecy at work. In the first half of the twentieth century Switzerland managed to stay out of both world wars, kept the exchange rate constant, and guaranteed that the Swiss franc remained freely convertible throughout the whole period. What better conditions could a country hope for in such times? Studer writes:

> Swiss bankers – invigorated by banking secrecy secured by Swiss law in 1934 – became known as trustworthy administrators who did not ask too many questions ... This rise of a financial centre, achieved in the first half of the twentieth century and followed by constant expansion of Swiss financial institutions, is believed to have brought prosperity not only to an ever growing service sector, but, by its sheer size and its links to other sectors, to the Swiss economy as a whole.

It still took time for the country's wealth to trickle down. While it is true that the Swiss economy as a whole improved early and was already among the world's most successful around 1900, as mentioned, up until the First World War Swiss workers lagged behind their counterparts in many other European countries. The national general strike of 1918 was a response to real grievances about the plight of workers. The strike, in which three protestors were killed, shook the establishment to the core and is still considered a major turning point in twentieth century Swiss history. Directly or indirectly, that taste of class warfare contributed to an improvement in wages and working conditions.

In his book about the secret of Switzerland's success, *Swiss Made*, R. James Breiding points out that Switzerland's rise to great prosperity was never planned: "There was no 'Swiss master plan', no sense of cultural mission, no Swiss ideology and all-embracing strategy imposed by a powerful government that evolved into a national formula for success."

While giving due weight to geographical, historical and political factors, Breiding attributes much of the country's success to the Swiss work ethic and sense of entrepreneurship, especially when combined with the contribution of immigrants and refugees over the centuries. The examples of immigrant success stories include Henri Nestlé, who was a German political refugee and Zino Davidoff, the Russian Jew whose name became a luxury brand. Leo Sternbach, the inventor of Valium and the saviour of Roche Pharmaceuticals, was a Polish refugee, and not to mention Ernesto Bertarelli, holder of Switzerland's fifth biggest family fortune, whose team twice sailed to victory in the America's Cup, is Italian-born.

But hard work isn't enough – it needs opportunity to bear fruit. The excellent apprenticeship system does just that; students who do not go down the university path are well-trained and well-respected. Not only do they emerge from three or four years years of vocational training with a good qualification, they can make a good living. The Swiss graphic designer, bank teller, florist or electrician has learned technical and business skills, and has access to further training. School leavers have around 300 registered apprenticeships to choose from in dual track vocational education and training programmes that combine one or two days of classroom based training with part-time training at the host company.

Those who wish to add to their qualifications after completing an apprenticeship have the option to enrol in tertiary level professional training and sit federal exams. This route provides professionals with highly technical or managerial training, with more than 50 study programmes available at colleges of higher education. This is why apprenticeships are also considered a good start to a business career. Many of Switzerland's top companies have been led by CEOs who started out as apprentices. Some of the best-known examples include Sergio Ermotti (UBS), Peter Meier (Kuoni) and Ernst Tanner (Lindt & Sprüngli).

Meanwhile, the importance of trade cannot be overlooked. It is still a key driver of Swiss prosperity. In the eighteenth century, Switzerland, with its strong textile industry, was the largest importer of cotton in continental Europe. Today, one Swiss company with eighteenth century roots, Paul Reinhart AG, has a 6% share of the world cotton market, according to Breiding. After getting off to a good start in the nineteenth century, Switzerland's industrial base continued to grow. Exports today account for 50% of the country's GDP, mainly medicinal and pharmaceutical products, watches and clocks, machinery for special industries and metalworking machinery and tools. Partly thanks to collective wage agreements in many sectors, Swiss workers are now among the best-paid in the world.

The other side of the coin

Let's go back to Tina Turner's party, which is now in full swing and beginning to annoy the neighbours. We had 135 millionaires in the crowd of 1,000 people. How about the poor? Using the Federal Statistics Office definition of the poverty line, 69 people at the party, (6.9% of the population) are living in poor households. This is a country where there are almost twice as many millionaires as poor people, which makes it all the harder to be short of money.

In Switzerland, "a person who does not have the financial means to acquire the goods and services they need to live a life integrated into society" is defined as living under the poverty line. One in thirteen Swiss residents fell into that category in 2012, a proportion that has been shrinking gradually in recent years. In a country where a cinema ticket costs 22 francs and a Big Mac will set you back 6.50 francs (the most expensive in the world, overvalued by 30% according to *The Economist*'s Big Mac index), a decent income is essential to be able to participate in everyday life.

Twice a year, for example, all Swiss car owners have to take their cars to a garage to change summer tyres to winter tyres and vice versa. The average price for this service is 95 francs, and a straightforward annual service may cost up to 800 francs. A filling at the dentist can set you back 180 francs. You can expect to pay 25 francs to get a key cut or buy a modest bunch of flowers. Health insurance is compulsory for all Swiss residents and the cheapest annual package for two adults and two children costs about 10,000 francs per year.

People in need, especially the elderly, are sometimes reluctant to ask for help from the authorities. Patrizia, a 33-year-old mother of two young children who works part-time at Zurich airport, does not earn enough to live securely but she refuses to apply for welfare. "I am fighting against becoming a welfare case. That is really important to me," she said in an interview with the Swiss charity Caritas. But why should the social welfare authorities inspire a sense of "panic-like fear" in someone like Patrizia who is entitled to help? This fear can be traced back to the harsh child welfare system that existed in Switzerland until the 1970s.

In the middle of the twentieth century, despite rising wages and a fast-growing economy, a significant proportion of the population lived in existential poverty, especially in rural areas. The standard response to families who got into financial difficulties was to take one or more children into care, with or without their parents' consent. Because the communes would have had to foot the bill for any financial support provided to poor families, the preferred solution was to send the child to a foster family or an institution.

Unfortunately for the children taken into care, the foster care system had inadequately evolved from a tradition of farmers taking on child servants. Markets for the annual hire of such children, organised by communes, continued up to the 1920s. By the end of the Second World War, a legal definition of the fostering arrangement was in place and a monthly sum was paid to foster families for the children's upkeep. However, the children were still seen as second-class citizens in the community. These were children from poor families, whose parents might be divorced, unmarried or have alcohol problems, triggering the intervention of the authorities. This stigma was passed on to the children. Added to their vulnerability, contact with the birth family was discouraged, and supervision was completely inadequate.

Roland Begert, taken into care shortly after his birth in the late 1930s, spent the first 12 years of his life in a children's home before being sent to live and work on a farm. When he went to find his legal guardian as an adult, the person he blamed for the lack of care and protection in his young years, the lawyer explained that he had guardianship of 300 children. He could not even manage to visit all his wards once a year, let alone arrange a good start in life for them.

Begert attended night school and managed to climb out of poverty, against all the odds, eventually qualifying as an economics teacher. He came to terms with his past by researching his case and writing a memoir. Many other individuals were unable to overcome the emotional scars of their early years, and have tried to keep their past a secret.

Until the late 1970s, if a pregnant woman was rejected by her family and the father of her child, it became practically impossible for her to raise her own child. This is what happened to Michèle Gillard, a woman in her 60s from the industrial town of La-Chaux-de-Fonds, who was sent to an orphanage when her parents' marriage broke up. As a young adult in 1970 under the guardianship of the authorities, her own first child was forcibly adopted. When she got pregnant again a few years later she did her best to keep under the radar. She found cheap accommodation and begged for food from restaurants, avoiding any contact with social services. Today Gillard and many more like her, with no training and a mixed employment background, live under the poverty line.

After a decade of awareness-raising and campaigning by former victims, stories like these are now familiar to the Swiss public. Many former foster children and institutionalised children number among the poor of Switzerland today, a reminder of a dark chapter in Swiss social history. Close to 1,000 victims who have come forward have been paid compensation from a provisional compensation fund set up by campaigners for justice, but a statutory compensation programme was established, thanks to pressure from campaigners, under which victims will be entitled to a set payment of between 20,000 and 25,000 francs in compensation. The government estimated that 12,000 to

15,000 survivors of harsh treatment under the old care regime could benefit but far fewer people applied to the scheme.

These life-long poor are joined by people whose standard of living drops after a marriage break-up, those not fit to work due to illness or disability, and immigrants who have not managed to gain a foothold in Swiss society. The lowest state payments for pensioners, disabled people and asylum seekers are around 1,100 francs per month for a single person. Means-tested rent and health insurance subsidies are also available. Homelessness also exists in Switzerland, but the number of people sleeping rough is estimated to be in the hundreds rather than thousands. In Geneva, two civil protection shelters, built as nuclear bunkers, are opened in the winter to cater for people with nowhere else to go. Some 1,100 people stayed there in the five-month period up to March 2017. In addition to people having to sleep on the streets or in shelters, there is the problem of hidden homelessness – people living with friends and relatives who are struggling to find affordable accommodation. A charity in the city of Basel that offers a postal address to people without a fixed address had more than 600 people registered for the service in 2014.

Minimum wage and unemployment
We're back on the shore of Lake Zurich, and Tina Turner's party is over. Some of the millionaires live within walking distance; the rest have rushed off to catch the last tram, along with the other guests. A few middle class stragglers, too slow to make the tram, weigh up spending some of their €25,745 disposable income on a taxi. Anticipating a big clean-up, the caterer has tracked down some cleaners among the guests and asked them to do an hour's work at the end the night. Ms Turner needs her sleep. The cleaners are low-paid workers belonging to the bottom earning 10% of the Swiss workforce.

Three-quarters of voters rejected the initiative, and turnout was considered high at 55%

When the Swiss were asked to vote on the introduction of a minimum wage in 2014, the rest of the world did a double take. The hourly rate being proposed – 22 francs (then $25 or €18) – seemed astoundingly high. For someone working the standard 42-hour week in Switzerland, it added up to a gross monthly salary of 4,000 francs.

Compare this amount to the minimum wage in place in other European countries. Some 22 European Union countries have statutory national minimum wages. At the beginning of 2015, Germany introduced a minimum hourly wage of €8.50. The rate in the EU ranges from €11.10 in Luxembourg to €1.04 in Bulgaria. The federal minimum wage in the United States is just USD 7.25 per hour ($1.00 was worth €0.85 at the time of writing).

Voters rejected the initiative, swayed perhaps by the argument that the change was not necessary, given that 95% of employees were already earning at least that amount, many thanks to collective wage agreements in the different sectors.

Swiss voters are generally loath to curb the freedom of businesses to make their own decisions. A year before the minimum wage vote, they rejected another initiative requiring a cap to be imposed on top-level management salaries. If that initiative had passed, top managers would not have been allowed to earn more than twelve times the amount earned by their lowest paid employees.

A spell of unemployment in most countries comes with a high risk of slipping into poverty. Not necessarily in Switzerland. To start with, as a rule, no one can be fired from one day to the next. The period of notice ranges from one month to three months, depending on length of service with the employer. Rarely rising above 3.5%, the Swiss unemployment rate is low enough to make other European countries weep with envy. The unemployment insurance system is generous by any standards. The jobless are entitled to receive 70 to 80% of their previous salary (up to a maximum of 10,500 francs per month) from the unemployment fund. The unemployment centre assists and monitors them in their job hunt and provides training to improve their prospects or job-seeking skills where necessary.

Most people are back at work within 12 months before having to transfer to other regular (usually lower) social welfare payments.

One Swiss scheme to keep workers' incomes stable in a downturn has proved very useful in preventing redundancies. Under the short-time working system, a company that sees its orders fall can temporarily switch some of its employees to part-time hours. The missing income is mostly made up by the unemployment fund and, in theory, the workers can be put back on full hours when business improves. The metalworking sector has had to rely on this scheme in recent years, as it has suffered more than most under the strong franc.

Spending it

A big topic of conversation at Tina Turner's party (and every Swiss party) is holidays. Of the 1,000 guests, half have cars, 85 own second homes and 913 in total are able to afford at least one annual holiday. This is high compared to Germany, where 22% of the population has to do without a proper break, and Britain, where one third of the population live in a household that cannot afford a week away.

So what does the average family earn and how do they spend their income? An imaginary average family with 1.5 children earns just over 10,000 francs per month. Some 570 francs of that goes on holiday expenses, adding up to almost 7,000 per year. A quarter of their income goes to social security deductions, tax and compulsory health insurance, while 1,500 francs is spent on housing and energy.

The majority of Swiss households live in rented accommodation. In fact, the Swiss have the lowest home ownership rate in Western Europe, at less than 34%. This may seem odd given the economic strength of the country, but there are disincentives to buy, such as a high deposit requirement (up to 30%), high property prices, and tax on imputed rental (Swiss home-owners have to pay tax on the rental value of their property, as if they were actually earning that rental income, even when they live in the house themselves). Strong legal protection for tenants and the availability of high quality rental housing also makes long-term renting attractive.

Monthly housing costs of 1,500 francs would seem low to people living in places like Zurich and Geneva, where rent on a three-room apartment costs on average 2,432 and 2,029 francs respectively. But the bulk of the population lives in cheaper areas, and low mortgage repayments thanks to low interest rates also bring down the average.

The average family budget also includes 750 francs per month for entertainment, recreation and culture – those trips to the cinema and some of the vast range of music festivals and concerts held in Switzerland.

With its abundance of well-qualified workers all expecting high salaries, the Swiss end up paying through the nose for goods and services. As the German journalist Wolfgang Koydl jokes in his book *Wer hat's erfunden? Unter Schweizer* (Who invented it? Among the Swiss): "Why are the Swiss so rich? Because they have to be."

There is a lot of political handwringing about *Hochpreisinsel Schweiz* (high-price island Switzerland). But despite years of headlines declaring that various parties "have the problem in their sights", no effective measures have yet been introduced to tackle high prices. Consumer organisations are hoping to force the government to act through an upcoming people's initiative. Many imported products are twice the price in Switzerland compared to neighbouring countries. It is no wonder that Swiss residents are tempted to cross the border for better deals. According to Credit Suisse calculations, Swiss retailers missed out on some 9.1 billion francs in sales in 2017, as thousands of Swiss residents made shopping pilgrimages to cheaper Germany or France. They return home, cars packed with clothes, meat and toiletries. To cater for Swiss who want to avoid custom duties on products ordered abroad, German farmers have set up in the package-reception business, using barns once used to store tractors to store packages from Amazon now.

One thing the Swiss don't have to spend money on is education. The state system is well-funded and well-trusted, so much so that it is considered eccentric to pay for private school. Imagine a country where there is no big discussion about where to send your child to school, no angst, no waiting lists and no moving house to get into the right street. Children are simply enrolled in the school for their catchment area and life goes on. University tuition is relatively low at 1,000 to 4,000 francs per year.

The Swiss do like to spend money on their hobbies. Switzerland has the highest level of motorbike ownership per capita in Europe with 425,000 motorbike riders on the road. On a fine day the hills are alive with the sound of horsepower. From wine collecting to beer-making, the Swiss pour money into their passions, and you will often find the evidence in their basements. A former colleague of mine has a collection of dozens of vintage juke boxes. The standard ice-breaker on the first visit to someone's home is to be shown around the house. Your host will open a door beside the laundry room, flick on the lights and stand back a little sheepishly while you admire, say, an array of equipment sufficient to set up a small recording studio.

Much as they like to spend, the Swiss are also very keen on saving, whether for a rainy day or retirement. The average Swiss household has 171,000 francs in savings. And saving starts young in Switzerland. If Sleeping Beauty had been Swiss, the fairy godmothers who attended her christening would definitely have opened a bank account for the new-born princess. Among the display of children's birthday cards in a store, you will find cards with small envelopes integrated into the design. These pockets are big enough for a note folded into quarters. The smallest denomination note that exists in Switzerland is 10 francs, a good place to start on the road to 171,000 francs.

The Swiss are, by any measure, a rich nation, and the strong franc has given them enviable buying power abroad. They could in theory purchase that Tuscan villa, if it weren't for the fact that savings in Switzerland are sacrosanct. But somehow, in their own country, they don't feel so rich. The combination of a high cost of living and high expectations quickly empties the wallets of the middle class, leaving them wondering at the end of the month – where did it all go?

In focus: Cats served with white wine and garlic
This is a book that aims to test the myths or widely held beliefs about Switzerland. There is one myth about Switzerland that is such a distortion of the facts, it is meowing out to be debunked.

If you are a reader of BBC news online, *The Washington Post*, *The Scotsman*, *Newsweek*, *The Huffington Post*, *The Times*, Australia's *ABC online* or the *Daily Mail*, you may be under the impression that cat meat is a favoured delicacy in Switzerland. Trying googling "Swiss eat ..." and the prompt "cats" will appear at the top of the list.

This story has legs: it first appeared in the early 1990s, sparked by a petition calling for a ban on the consumption of cat and dog meat, brought by a small animal rights group *Aktive Tierschutzgruppe Salez* or ATS (Active Animal Protection Group Salez). ATS was a one-woman operation led by animal rights activist Edith Zellweger, whose unsupported claims have run as news all over the world. Zellweger got 6,000 people to sign her petition, but the government declined to make private butchering of cats and dogs illegal, partly because it was such a non-issue and partly because it was viewed as a matter of personal choice.

So how has the practice of eating cats or dogs, seen all over Europe in times of famine, war or extreme poverty, become associated with the modern-day Swiss? It was the combination of an irresistibly nasty story and dogged campaigning on one side, met by lazy reporting at home and abroad on the other side, as Michael Breu, a journalist from the *Basler Zeitung* found out.

In 1994, after the story had taken off, Breu went searching in Appenzell for evidence of "dogs for dinner" following a tip from ATS, and ended up like most of his colleagues from other Swiss news outlets at the same farm where dog meat was indeed available. This, along with some speculative comments by a local vet, had been taken as proof that the practice was widespread.

Interviewed by Swiss Public Radio as recently as 2013, Zellweger stood by her accusations, albeit regional in focus: "If I was to drive around inner Appenzell, I would find every second or third person eats dogs. It's the same in Rheintal [Canton St Gallen]. I think it's a scandal." Following the interview, the radio reporter went knocking on doors around the rural area in question and found one person who admitted having eaten dog 20 years previously, and a farmer in his 80s who said he had butchered several dogs over the years. The farmer did not see the reason for the fuss, he had eaten dog meat as a child because his family was poor.

Then in 2014, a new campaigner stepped into the breach, bringing the story back to life in spectacular fashion. Thanks to completely unsubstantiated claims made by Tomi Tomek, founder and president of the Swiss animal protection association *SOS Chats Noiraigue*, it was reported worldwide, led by the news agency AFP, that 3% of the Swiss population – hundreds of thousands of people – regularly ate cat meat, often at Christmas and preferably in a stew with white wine and garlic. With a special interest in cats, Tomek had launched a petition calling for a ban on the consumption of cat meat, collecting 16,000 signatures.

When questioned by the more sceptical journalists about the 3% claim, Tomek said she had first heard it from a journalist, and that it also had been confirmed by the Federal Veterinary Office. The federal office dismissed the claim out of hand. "I have no idea where this figure comes from but definitely not from us," a spokeswoman told *20 Minuten* newspaper in November 2014.

Too late! The news stories about the hundreds of thousands of cat-and-dog-eating Swiss had already departed and are still circulating online in many languages on the websites of some of the most respected global media outlets. So the idea lives on. Even a slickly-produced spoof video in English that emerged as recently as February 2016 showing a fictitious Swiss master chef preparing a "favourite cat dish of his grandmother's" managed to fool many viewers as it spread widely on social media, and was tentatively picked up by some news websites. It turned out to have been produced by anti-meat-eating activists, Beyond Carnism, who let the public outrage build up before they identified themselves.

I have to leave it there, folks. I've got something on the stove.

CHAPTER 3

The Swiss Are Xenophobic

"Do you know why Italians are so small?" Bern city president Alexander Tschäppät asked at a comedy event in 2013. "Because their mothers always say to them: When you're big you'll have to go and work."

His stand-up routine got a lot of comic mileage out of the cliché of "southern" laziness: "A Neapolitan who works too much? That's so contradictory. It's like me saying there was such a thing as a nice Mörgeli [a political rival]." Italians, who first arrived in Switzerland in significant numbers in the 1950s and 1960s as economic migrants, are still the country's largest immigrant group. One in four Swiss residents is foreign-born, by far the highest proportion of immigrants living in a European country (excluding tiny Luxembourg), compared to 13% in the UK and less than 1% in Poland, or even 13% in the USA, famous for accepting "your poor, your huddled masses".

And yet Tschäppät is no Donald Trump, no Marine le Pen, but a member of the Social Democrats. Sure enough, he became a laughing stock himself when his lame jokes hit the headlines: "Embarrassing city president: Tschäppät makes jokes about Italians," the straight-laced Zurich-based *NZZ* wrote: "Tschäppät under fire over foreigner jokes," ran the headline in the *Blick* tabloid. Tschäppät pleaded comedic immunity, issuing a classic non-apology through a spokesman. "Most people can distinguish between a comedy appearance and a serious political appearance. If I hurt the feelings of some individuals, then I regret that."

But such mild xenophobia in the form of crude stereotyping of foreign nationalities is common in Switzerland, although it can occasionally go much further. After a stabbing in Interlaken in 2011, the Swiss People's Party placed an ad in several newspapers with the caption "Kosovars slash Swiss people" over an illustration showing black-booted feet (signifying immigrants) marching across the Swiss flag. "If you don't want this, sign the popular initiative 'Stop mass immigration' now", the ad declared. Two senior party members were later convicted of breaching an anti-racism law and fined.

A weekly current affairs magazine, *Die Weltwoche*, caused a furore in April 2012 with its cover photo of a small Roma child pointing a gun at the camera. The magazine has ties to the right wing Swiss People's Party; its editor, Roger Köppel, successfully ran for parliament as a People's Party candidate in 2015. The cover headline made a clear link between so-called gypsies and crime: "The Roma are coming: Plundering in Switzerland." The writer claimed he was only describing a real phenomenon of "crime tourism" and child abuse by Roma gangs. The Swiss Press Council ruled that *Die Weltwoche* had breached media ethics with its use of the little boy's image.

According to the prevailing clichés, people from former Yugoslavia are thugs; the Portuguese stick to themselves and don't learn the language; North Africans are thieves; black Africans are drug dealers; and Muslims are a security threat. While these clichés might be demoralising for the foreign population, negating their valuable contribution to Swiss society, for politicians they are a political goldmine. In the last decade there have been seven initiatives related to immigration, asylum or foreign criminals and each has tapped into the emotions summoned by these clichés.

Meine Scheidung: Ein Hausmann über den gescheiterten Rollentausch

Nummer 14 · 5. April 2012 · 80. Jahrgang
Fr. 6.50 (inkl. MwSt.) · Euro 4.40

DIE WELTWOCHE

Die Roma kommen: Raubzüge in die Schweiz

Familienbetriebe des Verbrechens.
Von Philipp Gut und Kari Kälin

Die unsichtbare Schlinge

Wie Staatsverträge Schweizer Recht aushebeln. *Von Urs Paul Engeler*

Casanova, der Intellektuelle

Der weltberühmte Liebhaber war eigentlich ein Mann des Geistes.
Von Tony Perrottet

The 5 April 2012 *Weltwoche* cover: "The Roma are Coming: Plundering in Switzerland"

Does this mean the Swiss are xenophobic? I believe it's more the case that the xenophobic Swiss feel free to express their opinions publicly. In the lead up to the 2014 soccer World Cup, there were grumblings about there being too many foreign-born or second-generation immigrants in the Swiss national football team. The issue became a public talking point after it was raised by one of the players, Stephan Lichtsteiner. The most widely read (and free) Swiss newspaper *20 Minuten* carried an interview with Lichtsteiner with the following introduction:

> The current national team is mostly made up of *Secondos* [naturalised second-generation immigrants]. Only 10 players in the 23-man team … are Swiss without a migration background. And since the summer of 2014, the national team also has a trainer that doesn't see himself only as Swiss, but by his own admission as a Bosnian Croat (born in Sarajevo). Are there not enough Swiss people in Switzerland? Can it even be called a Swiss national team? It is no secret that this theme is being controversially discussed in the whole country.

Lichtsteiner uses "Swiss" in its narrow sense: having no migration background. Though Lichtsteiner praised his teammates who are not pure Swiss as "great guys and super footballers", he tried to make the point that Swiss fans needed to see more of their own people in the team. "It is important for me what happens with the national team. It is therefore also important for me that we take care of the so-called identification figures, because we don't really have too many of them left."

Some people suggested that certain players were only wearing the Swiss colours for cynical, self-serving reasons. On the positive side, the fact that so many children of foreigners are advancing through the ranks in Swiss football is a reflection of an inclusive system for fostering talent. The over-representation of immigrants or children of immigrants in the national team is most likely a class issue. As an inexpensive sport, football is traditionally an avenue for success for children from poorer backgrounds. Talented players with lots of other great opportunities tend to drop out of the gruelling training schedule.

Amid all the hot air spoken about foreigners, it is easy to lose sight of the fact that Switzerland, with one quarter of its population born abroad, is ticking along nicely with little or no social strife. Despite all the efforts to create a rift between the native population and other nationalities or ethnic groups, a solid majority of Swiss citizens remain tolerant, albeit in a less vocal way.

The issue of xenophobia is closely watched in Switzerland by bodies such as the State Secretariat for Migration, the Federal Commission Against Racism, and the Service for Combating Racism. A national study on racism and xenophobia, based on in-depth interviews carried out by social researchers gfs.bern between 2010 and 2014, found that one in four Swiss residents had xenophobic attitudes. Interestingly, the differences between results for Swiss nationals and non-nationals were dramatic (30% versus 5% with xenophobic attitudes). Xenophobic attitudes were measured in a variety of ways, such as how people felt about their neighbours, how freely they expressed their opinions in public, how they felt in the presence of "others", and what stereotypes or negative views they agreed with. It's difficult to get directly comparable studies in this area. A study in the United Kingdom in 2013 (British Social Attitudes survey) found that 29% of those surveyed said they had some level of prejudice against people other races.

If one quarter of the Swiss residents surveyed had xenophobic attitudes, that still leaves a comfortable majority of people who have no problem with the cultural mix in their communities. Three quarters of the Swiss population works and lives alongside other nationalities without harbouring any ill-will towards them.

For every person who answered yes to questions like: "Would you like there to be no Muslims in Switzerland?", "Should the practising of Islam be forbidden in Switzerland?" or "Should Muslims be prevented from immigrating here?", three to four people answered no. This majority does not automatically view different nationalities as criminals, layabouts or social welfare cheats. Thanks to tolerance, foreigners in Switzerland have been able to flourish. People whose own countries have failed to provide good prospects for them for political or economic reasons have found the land of opportunity or refuge here, among them great talents such as Albert Einstein, Charlie Chaplin and Nicolas Hayek, founder of Swatch.

It's not just the big name foreigners who have found success in Switzerland. A recent OECD report found that Switzerland was unusual in having far fewer immigrants working in jobs for which they were overqualified (17% as opposed to 32% OECD average). Children of immigrants were also less likely to experience discrimination. Only 5% of Swiss-born children of immigrants stated that they had been discriminated against. The EU average was above 20%. Meanwhile foreigners are increasingly taking over the reins in the top Swiss companies. When Credit Suisse chose a black African, French Ivorian Tidjane Thiam, as its new chief executive in 2015, the decision was applauded by the Swiss media. Thiam is just one example of the readiness of the Swiss to draw on foreign talent. Mark Branson, head of the Swiss Financial Regulatory Authority (Finma), an Englishman, rules over the financial sector in heavily accented German. Indeed, two thirds of the top managers in the 30 largest companies quoted on the Swiss stock exchange are now foreign citizens. Evidently, shareholders have a different idea of what it means to be Swiss than Lichtsteiner.

The argument that the Swiss will welcome anyone whose children can one day look and talk like them, but not Africans or Asians, is hard to prove or disprove. The fact is that immigrants from outside Europe comprise a small segment of the population. Reports of racist attacks are rare, although there were 380 prosecutions under the anti-racism law in the first

20 years of its existence since 1995. Actions that injure the human dignity of an individual or group or cross the line into incitement to hatred or propaganda are against the law. Most convicted offenders received fines or suspended fines. Much has been made of a 2013 incident when a Zurich shop clerk refused to show Oprah Winfrey a thirty-thousand-franc handbag, steering her towards a lower priced item, but that is surely no proof of institutionalised racism.

The truth is, negligible unemployment, low taxes, a well-functioning health service and good social services mean Swiss residents have less to complain about in their everyday lives. This leaves room to focus on other worries, such as the fear that the country is getting overcrowded, as seen in pressure on housing and public transport in particular. The issue has been centre stage since the Swiss population rose above the eight million mark in 2012. Urban sprawl is an increasing problem in the densely populated central plateau region where most of the eight million live. The population doubled over the twentieth century and in recent years the growth rate has been above 1% per year. Immigration is the main driver of this growth, but the Swiss have not resorted to Pegida (Patriotic Europeans Against the Islamisation of the West)-style anti-immigrant marches that mushroomed in Germany in 2014–15, because disgruntled Swiss citizens have the power to directly influence immigration policy at the ballot box. We'll come back to *Ausländerpolitik*, the never-ending political battles over how to deal with the foreign population, later in the chapter.

Who are Switzerland's foreigners?

Switzerland is full of accidental foreigners: people who have come to Switzerland more as a response to push and pull factors than as part of a long-term plan. Excluding Luxembourg, Switzerland's 25% foreigner head count is by far the highest proportion in any European country (the share of non-national residents in most EU countries is below 10%), an oft quoted fact that helped convince Swiss voters in 2014 to limit the freedom of European Union citizens to come and work in Switzerland after more than a decade of maintaining a two-way open labour market.

As mentioned, immigration in Switzerland is largely a European phenomenon. Switzerland shares borders with four large countries inhabited by people speaking the same languages as the Swiss. Taking into account that people are more and more prepared to move long distances to find work, and that the buoyant Swiss job market has openings for high-salaried positions with the chance to work in three different languages, it is little wonder that the country has attracted so many foreign "cousins". Citizens from these neighbouring countries – Italy, Germany, France and Austria – account for 40% of the Swiss foreign population. Other European nationalities make up another 40% of the total, led by Portugal (13.1%), Kosovo (5.8%), Spain (4.0%) and Serbia (3.9%). Six per cent of foreigners hail from Asian countries and around the 4% mark (ca. 80,000 people) are groups from African countries, North America and Turkey.

These numbers include the Swiss-born children of immigrants who have not been naturalised, indistinguishable from their Swiss classmates and colleagues in all but their parents' cooking and the colour of their passports. The Swiss have historically kept the bar to citizenship relatively high, in some part out of fear of being overrun by foreigners. The process of naturalisation is slow, expensive and designed to be intimidating, often involving an interview in front of a panel of officials and possibly language and citizenship tests. The result is a self-selection dynamic that means low-income households with a low level of education are underrepresented among applicants.

The irony is that in clinging to the ideal that Swiss citizenship has to be hard won, the Swiss have created an artificially-foreign generation, endangering the loyalty and affection of those would-be Swiss.

Different strokes for different folks
The best measure of xenophobia is to ask the people on the receiving end how they feel. In Switzerland, as in other countries, your experience depends on whether you are seen as a good foreigner or a bad foreigner. There are different ways to qualify as a good foreigner in Switzerland, from the Swiss viewpoint. Ideally you should have lived here for a long time and speak one of the local languages. But it's not enough to be law abiding and hard-working yourself; your nationality also needs to have a good reputation. In Swiss crime reporting, it is common practice for the nationality of the offender or arrested person to be mentioned. Even naturalised Swiss citizens have their previous nationality reported.

There's a welcome on the mat if you're married to a Swiss, as long as there's no hint of you having been motivated by needing a residence permit. That makes you a bad foreigner. If you must be Muslim, try not to appear too religious. For every foreigner, a touch of humility goes a long way, some sign that you appreciate your good fortune at having ended up in Switzerland. Oh, and if you've arrived in the past five years, best not to be an asylum seeker.

Germans may not seem terribly foreign to the outsider's eye or ear, but to the Swiss the difference is crucial because not being German is a central element of Swiss German identity. If they cannot maintain this distinction from their dominant neighbour, what becomes of their Swissness? Speaking humble dialects of a great language is both a source of pride and embarrassment to the Swiss. Pedro Lenz is an award-winning

Swiss author who writes in dialect. When I met him in Bern to discuss his book *Der Goalie Bin Ig*, translated into Glaswegian dialect under the title *Naw Much of a Talker*, he admitted he used to have a complex about the German language. It was only after spending time in Glasgow and getting to know Scottish authors writing in Glaswegian dialect that he had the courage to get over this complex and attempt to write in his own voice. He hasn't looked back. *Der Goalie Bin Ig* was his first book written in dialect, and it went on to be a best-seller.

Anti-German sentiment is not unknown in other European countries. However, in Switzerland it has appeared as a response to immigration rather than to any bitterness over world wars. The influx of Germans since the economic downturn in the European Union has not gone unnoticed in Swiss work places, particularly in academia and medicine.

The *Berner Zeitung* reported in November 2015 that 5,900 of the 30,000 doctors practising in Switzerland were German, up from 4,200 five years earlier. The percentage in hospitals, as opposed to private practice, is much higher. The figures appeared in a story featuring Swiss doctors' complaints that Germans in senior positions were favouring their own compatriots when recruiting.

"Swiss doctors' fears are justified," said Hans-Ueli Würsten of the Association of Senior Swiss Hospital Physicians *(Verein der Leitenden Spitalärzte Schweiz)*. "Every time a German doctor gets a management position in a Swiss hospital, a murmur goes through the medical team." Würsten claimed to know German hospital managers who openly admitted that they only hired assistant doctors from Germany.

In a 2015 Vienna University of Economics and Business study, half of the German immigrants interviewed viewed their nationality as a disadvantage in Switzerland. A third tried to disguise their German identity by speaking less or not at all.

A tale of two professors

In February 2014, by the slimmest of majorities (50.3%), Swiss voters accepted a right wing proposal to impose immigration quotas on European Union citizens coming to live and work in Switzerland, after more than a decade of maintaining a two-way open labour market between Switzerland and the EU. The anti-immigration vote was the last straw for Christoph Höcker, an archaeologist who had been teaching at the Institute for History and Theory of Architecture at top university ETH Zurich since 1999. Höcker wrote an email to his students announcing his resignation in bitter terms. "We keep reading in the comments section of the Tagi [*Tages-Anzeiger* newspaper]," wrote Höcker, "that the Germans should just disappear. Now that's what I'm doing. I've resigned, and I'm sure that some farm boy from Obwalden can take my place teaching the course." The incident was widely reported, with the *20 Minuten* newspaper quoting Höcker in its headline, "A lower salary in exchange for not being marginalised any more."

The professor obviously took the immigration vote as a personal affront. But while lashing out at the Swiss, he also revealed a touch of German snobbishness, the very characteristic the Swiss, with their country bumpkin dialect, are so sensitive about. Höcker also urged German doctors and nurses to return home: "If the Swiss don't want us, then they should see how they get on without us."

Perhaps some did follow Höcker's example but by the end of 2014 there were 6,000 more Germans living in Switzerland than a year before, bringing the total German population to 298,000.

In its commentary on the high figures for foreign residents, the Federal Statistics Office attributes those high numbers to large waves of immigration, a restrictive naturalisation policy and the fact that foreigners have more children and, being younger than the Swiss population, fewer deaths. The naturalisation question leads us to the story of another underappreciated foreign professor, Irving Dunn. An American citizen married to a German, Dunn came to Switzerland in 1970 and has lived in the commune of Einsiedeln in Canton Schwyz for 40 years. A village within commuting distance of Zurich, Einsiedeln is a lovely place, famous for its Benedictine monastery with the Black Madonna, a pilgrimage site which attracts tens of thousands of tourists every year. In October 2014 it was in the spotlight for an incomprehensible act of exclusion against a long-term resident.

Because every citizen of Switzerland is also a citizen of their canton and commune (municipality), applications for naturalisation must be approved at three levels – federal, cantonal and communal. As part of the direct democracy tradition, every commune still has the right to accept or reject an application for citizenship. In some communes, this can be done by a show of hands at a general assembly open to all the citizens. In fact, the Federal Court ruled against secret ballot voting in 2003 following a scandal involving the commune of Emmen, a suburb of Lucerne, which was found to be unjustly rejecting applicants from Balkan countries. In lieu of the open vote, many cantons appoint naturalisation commissions to review applications. These panels are commissioned to draw up reports for the federal and cantonal authorities and they wield the most power in the procedure.

In Dunn's case, his application was studied by a commission of six people who interviewed him, and their recommendation was put to an open vote at the general assembly of the commune. The commission found that Dunn didn't know the local area well enough, couldn't name local friends, and did not socialize in the village. He's not integrated, they told the audience, a serious fault because integration is a key requirement to qualify for naturalisation. In spite of his four decades in the country, professorship at a leading Swiss university, mastery of

German, and excellent knowledge of Swiss culture, at the general meeting, the commission recommended to the 200 people in attendance to reject Dunn's application. By a narrow majority, they did. This meant that, out of a population of around 9,000 eligible voters, some 100 people (half of those in attendance) who turned up to a mid-week community meeting were able to block Dunn's path to citizenship. Prejudice is an unpredictable force when power is concentrated in the hands of a few politically active citizens. At the same meeting the assembly approved applications from 16 other residents of Einsiedeln, including immigrants from Turkey, Serbia and Sri Lanka.

Dunn laughs a lot when he talks about this episode. There is no trace of bitterness. "I'm not very sensitive. I'm amused by the whole thing. I never really had any trouble with the Swiss. I've been very lucky here – terrific academic job, good students, lots of money."

He believes it may have bothered the commission that his wife didn't apply for citizenship with him. He found the interview quite patronizing, having to sit in front of six people and answer questions about local geography, his social life and friends. "I never said I didn't have friends in Einsiedeln. They asked me if I had good friends in the area and I took that to mean close friends."

Swiss naturalisation requirements are among the strictest in Europe. Applicants who are not spouses or children of Swiss citizens have to live in the country for 12 years before they can apply. Recipients of social welfare are not permitted to apply, nor is anyone with unpaid taxes or debts, and documents must be presented to prove this. Language proficiency and integration must be proven in a written test and or in-depth interviews or both. Under the facilitated procedure the spouse of a Swiss citizen may apply after five years, but it took me 11 years living in Switzerland before I finally filled in the form. I held back, not convinced it was the right move. What spurred me on was the desire to take my place among the Swiss on equal terms with voting rights. There were three main reasons for my initial reluctance, all personal but perhaps also universal. The first was the symbolic loss of my homeland, a painful reality which I felt would be formalised with this procedure. Secondly, pride came into play. Having lived here for a decade and contributed the fruits of my labour to this country for that time – my work output, my taxes, my social security contributions, a thousand supermarket trolleys full of produce, not to mention three new Swiss citizens, I felt that I had offered Switzerland a lot. A procedure that put me in the role of grateful supplicant, without any sense that the gratitude could extend both ways, was alienating to say the least. Finally, the exclusive workings of the whole procedure went against my values. Did I really want to call myself Swiss if it meant shutting the door on less "perfect" residents? I'm not alone. Only a small percentage (fewer than one in ten) of the foreigners living in Switzerland (including second and third generation immigrants) who would be eligible to apply for naturalisation actually do so. The reasons for that reluctance are complex, like everything in this country, but to some extent it's a standoff. Some bridge building would be helpful, but that's not what's happening on a political level.

Ausländerpolitik

The 1960s saw a large wave of guest workers from Italy, initially on temporary visas. To this day, the Italians are the largest immigrant group in Switzerland, numbering 316,500 people or 15% of the total immigrant population. They came in search of work, mainly from the south of Italy. Many hoped to save up and eventually return home when times were better. Life being the way it is, they settled where the work was, and became more and more tied to their children's first home. A strange outcome of restrictive naturalisation is that the children or grandchildren of these first generation of immigrants can be deported if they are convicted of a serious crime. A repeat offender with Italian nationality was ordered to leave Switzerland in December 2014, despite being the child of Swiss-born parents, having lived all his life in Switzerland and having a Swiss wife. The man had been convicted of more than 20 offences, including robbery, theft, and breaking and entering, as well as drug and gun offences. Clearly no country would want him as a citizen, but the Swiss political and legal system is obstinate enough to construct a false reality in which someone who is a product of Swiss society is classed as an Italian problem.

One name older immigrants will remember is Schwarzenbach. Son of a wealthy Swiss family, James Schwarzenbach embraced Nazi ideology as a young man in the 1930s. In later life he went on to represent the newly-formed anti-immigrant party *Nationale Aktion* in parliament in the 1960s. The highlight of his career was the popular initiative he spearheaded in 1970 which used the term *Überfremdung* (excess of foreignness). The post-war economic boom had brought one million new people into Switzerland, mainly from Southern Europe. The proposal before voters was to restrict immigrants to 10% of the total population, a constitutional change which, if introduced, would have meant the deportation of 300,000 people. When the Swiss were given the opportunity to vote yes or no to immigration – an option that didn't exist in most other countries – they flocked to the polling stations. The vote saw a historic high turnout of 75%. The initiative narrowly failed.

The Italian connection
At the time of the vote, Teodoro and Maddalena Potenza were recent arrivals from southern Italy. Like many immigrants, they thought they would stay a few years, make some money

and go back home. But more than 50 years on, they still live in Switzerland, close to their children and grandchildren. I went to visit the Potenzas in their home in a small village in Canton Fribourg. The Italian news was on the television when I arrived. The decor of their apartment had an Italian feel – the tiled floor, dark, heavy furniture – and the coffee was strong too. Teodoro remembers driving around Bern with some Italian friends on the day of the Schwarzenbach vote, waving an Italian flag out the window.

"We were just messing around," he said, laughing at the recollection. "The atmosphere wasn't nice then. But we were young, and we didn't let it bother us. If it's really bad, we thought, we'll go back. I personally did not feel unwelcome."

The couple experienced some challenges in the early years of their life in Switzerland but managed to make a good life for themselves. "It was difficult to get accommodation. You had to get a reference or approval from a Swiss before they would give you the contract. Sometimes we were called gypsies, and another name *'cinque li'* [*Tschingg* in Swiss German], after an Italian card game," Teodoro remembers.

Maddalena found factory work and Teodoro worked as a mechanic in the same garage for 40 years and spoke highly of his employer. "I found good work, a good boss and good money."

These days, though still Italian citizens, they can't deny they have become a bit Swiss. "After two weeks in Italy I want to come back," Maddalena said. "It's so quiet here, so nice. The noise bothers me in Italy. I couldn't live there any more. And the whole *raccomandazione* thing [getting ahead through connections]. Here everyone is equal."

This fear of *Überfremdung* still quickens the pulse of some Swiss. The idea of a putting a percentage ceiling on immigration has come up again, most recently in November 2014 when the so-called Ecopop initiative sought to limit growth to 0.2%

of net population, although voters have never accepted absolute limits (see Chapter 4).

Swiss citizens with xenophobic feelings have numerous channels to express their unease or outrage about the presence of so many foreigners in society. They can make spiteful comments online, either in social media or in the comments sections of newspapers. This is an outlet enjoyed by people from all walks of life, as long as they don't cross the line into incitement to hatred or racial discrimination, in which case they can be prosecuted. Therefore, it is all right to say: "Muslims are not wanted in Switzerland", but not all right to tweet: "We should have a new *Kristallnacht* for the Muslims", as a Swiss People's Party local politician from Zurich did in 2012. The published message was found to have breached anti-racism law, and the man was fined and publicly vilified for his action. Despite deleting the offensive tweet five minutes after posting it, the man lost his job, his party membership and political office, and his social network, according to his lawyer.

Resentment or distrust of foreigners can be expressed in more practical ways. In places like Einsiedeln, citizens can vote to keep individual foreigners out of the Swiss club. Swiss landlords may decline to rent out an apartment to people of certain nationalities, and employers may refuse to employ them. The Constitution includes a general ban on discrimination, but Switzerland does not have an anti-discrimination law at the federal level. The European Commission Against Racism and Intolerance has repeatedly called on Switzerland to introduce laws to clearly define and expressly prohibit direct and indirect racial discrimination. "This prohibition should apply to all public authorities and all natural and legal persons, whether active in the public or the private sector. It should encompass in particular the fields of employment, housing, goods and services intended for the public and access to public places."

More likely to come first is a law requiring employers to favour Swiss residents (albeit including foreign-nationals) when recruiting. The 2014 vote curbing EU immigration included this provision, with exceptions allowed in sectors experiencing a skills shortage.

Best of all, Swiss people nursing anti-foreigner sentiment can consistently vote on a national level to make life awkward for foreigners. Policy on foreigners is the perennial theme in Swiss politics, and, to stay in the game, every party has a detailed platform on the various issues. Swiss voters have had ample opportunity to influence that policy to the extent that the more centrist parties now describe themselves as "tough but fair" on foreigners.

The Swiss political system has a very special role for petitions. Under the initiative system, any citizen may call for a national vote on any issue or challenge a parliamentary decision, providing they collect at least 100,000 signatures (or 50,000 signatures for the latter, see Chapter 10) in support of their cause.

We all have our pet peeves, but not everyone has the resources to gather 50,000–100,000 signatures and get the nation to back them up. The result is that more often direct democracy is used by well-organised and well-funded lobby groups and political parties. The gold medal in this category goes to the right-wing Swiss People's Party. With more than a quarter of the popular vote, it is a fairly easy task for the party to gather so many signatures.

In December 2015, Swiss People's Party members participated in an information workshop in the parliament building in Bern for right-wing members of the European parliament organised by the Brussels-based Institute for Direct Democracy in Europe (IDDE), a foundation which describes itself as a think tank. The executive director of IDDE, Laure

Ferrari, a close ally of the Britain's Nigel Farage, ran in the 2014 European elections as a candidate for the right-wing French party *Debout la France* (Arise France). The Bern event was attended by members of Farage's UK Independence Party (UKIP), the Sweden Democrats, the Czech Free Citizen's Party, and the Lithuanian Order and Justice Party who wanted to find out whether the Swiss model of non-EU membership was exportable.

Asked about the cost of staging a referendum, Swiss People's Party politician Yves Nidegger told the group: "You have to consider that every signature that is collected and checked is going to cost you about €5 (CHF 5.4), so if you want 100,000 signatures, you need half a million [euros] to start. And later on, if you succeed, more to campaign," the international news service of the Swiss Broadcasting Corportation, *swissinfo.ch*, reported.

Using this financial and political clout, the Swiss People's Party has concentrated much of its resources on targeting foreigners.

In 2003, the Swiss People's Party campaigned against a proposal to make the naturalisation procedure easier for second and third generation foreigners, which included a provision for grandchildren of immigrants to be born Swiss, a step too far for a country whose view of nationality is shaped by a tradition of *jus sanguinis*, citizenship by blood, and not *jus solis*, citizenship by place of birth (soil). A 'No' campaign poster depicted hands of different colours grabbing at a box of Swiss passports.

Six years later, in 2009, the Swiss People's Party secured a ballot box ban on the construction of minarets. The Swiss Muslim population at the time was 7%. The main campaign poster showed a female figure in a black burqa in the foreground and the Swiss flag covered in giant black minarets in the background.

Different versions of this poster have been used in several campaigns over the past decade. This original version reads: "For more security / My home – our Switzerland."

In 2010, voters approved the automatic deportation of foreign criminals. This campaign featured the infamous black sheep poster, first seen when the deportation campaign was launched in the run up to the 2007 general election. The poster, commissioned by the Swiss People's Party, showed three cartoon sheep kicking one black sheep off the Swiss flag. This single poster got massive international media coverage, and did more to seal the Swiss reputation for xenophobia than any other single incident in recent years.

February 2014 saw a wafer-thin majority saying yes to reintroducing immigration quotas for EU citizens, signalling the end of 12 years of free movement of labour between Switzerland and the EU. The two most widely used People's Party posters showed a tree bearing fruit with its black roots piercing through a Swiss flag and large black boots walking over the flag. Turnout was considered high at 55.8%.

Refugees

In this context, almost unnoticed, the sympathy that was once felt for asylum seekers has gradually drained away, and any change to asylum law is framed as a necessary "tightening" to clamp down on abuse. In early 2016, Swiss national television reported that Syrian asylum seekers were being asked to hand over any cash above 1,000 francs. The Swiss State Secretariat for Migration said the regulation had only affected a small number of asylum seekers, 112 of the 39,500 who arrived in 2015. Following the upheaval of the Arab Spring and the massive displacement of people caused by the war in Syria, the Swiss share the fear of the rest of Europe that, should the continent take a sympathetic stance, Europe's security and relative prosperity would be threatened by the sheer numbers of people in need. The response in most countries is to turn a deaf ear to the cries of suffering. It wasn't always so.

In October and November 1956, Hungarians rose up against the Soviet-backed puppet government and for a few short weeks it looked as if there really could be a chink in the Iron Curtain. Then the Soviets sent in their tanks, crushed the uprising and started executing people. In the middle of all this turmoil, 200,000 Hungarians fled the country, many of them ending up in refugee camps in neighbouring Austria.

Ernest Horvath, a retired insurance executive from Zurich, was a small boy in one of those camps. His dramatic story illustrates the accidental nature of such journeys. Ernest's father worked in a garage and had access to a truck. Rumours were flying around about arrests and people who had managed to leave the country. In an atmosphere of fear and uncertainty, the Horvaths, along with three colleagues and their families, decided to make a break for the border. Now or never, they thought. They drove for several hours but when they got to no-man's land there were both Hungarian and Soviet soldiers on duty. Austria was within sight, just a few hundred metres away, but the families were terrified. No one knew what the soldiers might do to stop the refugees. Ernest remembers his father telling him to run, and he ran. But two of the families in the group lost their nerve at the last second. They did not dare to run at the critical moment, and they missed their chance, returning to the abandoned truck and several more decades of life under Communism.

There was a great outpouring of sympathy for the Hungarian refugees across Western Europe. Ernest's parents and their friends had been hoping to get to the United States, but when Switzerland offered to take a contingent of 14,000 refugees from the Austrian camps, they gladly accepted the Swiss resettlement offer. In November 1956, they climbed aboard a train headed west, and were stripped and deloused by Swiss matrons in a reception camp at the border. On the next leg of the journey, by chance, their train carriage was allocated to French-speaking Neuchâtel, where they were greeted on arrival with smiles and chocolate bars by the locals.

There was no hope of going back, which meant the new arrivals put all their energy into making a good life in Switzerland. Arriving on the cusp of an economic boom, the Hungarians, who were welcomed with open arms as victims of Communism, became model immigrants. Ernest went on to become a successful insurance executive. "I had a much more interesting life here with Swiss freedom and real democracy. I have every reason to be happy."

Switzerland accepted contingents of refugees again from Czechoslovakia (11,000) in 1968 and from Vietnam (8,000) in the late 1970s and early 1980s. Some 30,000 people found refuge in Switzerland during the 1992–1995 Bosnian war and a further 50,000 during the 1998–1999 Kosovo war. Today around 100,000 Kosovars live in Switzerland, and they may be the most critically-viewed immigrant group. In the xenophobia survey commissioned by the Service for Combating Racism, only 26% of Swiss said they could imagine working with an Albanian (largest ethnic group in Kosovo), the lowest popularity score of all.

In recent years, growing numbers of asylum seekers have made it to Switzerland from Eritrea, from the Arab Spring countries of North Africa, and from Syria. Bottlenecks have arisen in the asylum processing system, as well as not-in-my-backyard protests in communes where federal authorities try to establish asylum centres. There was uproar in the Fribourg commune of Giffers in early 2015 when it was announced that the federal authorities had bought a former boarding school called Guglera to use as an asylum centre. The night of the public information meeting locals lit bonfires on the hillsides and the representatives from Bern were shouted down when they tried to speak.

Soon afterwards I went to meet the owner of the Guglera property, set in the middle of rolling countryside, who had created all the fuss by selling it. Beat Fasnacht, who describes himself as a social entrepreneur, is a friendly giant in his late 60s. Used to being seen as the good guy locally, the information meeting was a tough experience for him. But he said he had received many supportive calls and messages since then. Fasnacht was running a residential training programme in Guglera for obese young people, helping them to attain a healthy lifestyle and get started on their careers, but there were funding difficulties. He felt the setting and the facilities would be ideal for asylum seekers: "We are all in one boat in this world."

Fresh asylum legislation, approved by parliament in 2015, set a maximum of 140 days for processing the majority of asylum requests. Asylum seekers are not permitted to work in Switzerland and are expected to live on a tiny cash allowance, leading to problems of idleness and petty crime. But even the Christian Democrats want to make Switzerland less attractive to asylum seekers, calling for vouchers to be given instead of cash, work programmes for no pay and travel restrictions. Asylum seekers are firmly stuck at the bottom of the foreigners' ladder for the foreseeable future.

Melting pot

Individual experiences vary so much it is hard to decide whether it is the best of times or the worst of times for foreigners in Switzerland. Overall, I believe there is cause to be optimistic. Despite all the negative political rhetoric about *Überfremdung*, foreigners are being absorbed by Swiss society in an organic way.

Because of the diversity within the country, with dialects or languages and customs changing from canton to canton and valley to valley, the Swiss are well-practiced in dealing with difference. They know what it's like to feel foreign inside their own country and, with increasing mobility in the jobs market, many are familiar with the effort it takes to integrate across a language divide. This can make it easier for the outsider to find a place in Swiss society. They will not be alone in their difference.

Diversity is also the norm inside families: Roger Federer with his South African mother, Stan Wawrinka with his Czech grandfather. Half of Swiss citizens have one foreign grandparent. The Swiss are voting with their hearts; almost as many Swiss marry foreigners as marry fellow Swiss citizens (36% versus 47% in 2016). The parents of the dozen or so children who wait for the school bus every morning outside the community centre in my neighbourhood come from nine different countries of origin: Switzerland, Vietnam, Germany, Tunisia, France, Mauritius, Spain, Peru and Ireland. When it's raining, the children huddle together at the entrance of the building; when the weather is fine they play on the swings or swap secrets in groups of two or three. The only thing that's foreign to these children right now is xenophobia. Let's hope that much is here to stay.

In focus: The Swiss abroad

Before Switzerland was a land of immigration, it was a land of emigration, mainly in the nineteenth century. More than 80,000 Swiss joined the mass wave of European emigration to the United States in the 1880s alone. To protect emigrants, the Confederation set up a Federal Emigration Office in 1888 intended to monitor the occasionally dubious activities of emigration agencies. It continued in operation until 1953. These agencies placed the emigrants with economic colonisation projects, mainly in North and South America. By the 1930s, the Swiss economy was much improved and Swiss emigration to the US had slowed to a mere 5,500 for the decade.

To this day there are Swiss towns in North and South America, Swiss clubs all over the world and 17 Swiss schools in four continents which receive federal funding. Many Swiss schools have opened and closed over the years, responding to changing patterns of Swiss residency. Two schools in Egypt operated from the 1920s to 1970, a time of prosperity for Swiss companies based in the North African country. Two schools opened in Rio de Janeiro and Sao Paolo in the 1960s when major Swiss companies were established in Brazil, increasing the Swiss population there in a short space of time. The Organisation for the Swiss Abroad organises summer camps for children of the Swiss diaspora.

Not everyone set their sights on crossing the Atlantic. Switzerland also saw a steady stream of skilled workers and farmers emigrating to the Russian Empire. When the Revolution began in 1917 there were some 8,000 Swiss citizens living in Russia working in a wide range of occupations. While about half lived in either Moscow or St Petersburg, including a tutor of the Romanov children, others were scattered all over the empire. This incredible story of one Swiss-Russian family shows how important the link to the homeland can be.

Valy Wüthrich was the eldest of three children born between 1927 and 1931 in a small village in rural Russia near the city of Smolensk, 400 kilometres south west of Moscow. Her grandparents had emigrated from Switzerland in the 1860s, bought land and become modestly prosperous farmers. Her father, Eduard, born in 1886, was a cheesemaker and farmer, and the family lived in an eight-room wooden house surrounded by a grain store, threshing room, stables, stalls, sauna and vegetable gardens. Valy's memories of her early childhood are idyllic. Her brothers Gennadi and Leo only remembered hard times. As Soviet collectivisation gathered pace, the family were branded *Kulaks*, a class which suffered terrible persecution and was destined to be liquidated by Stalin. Bit by bit, land and livestock were confiscated from the Wüthrichs until they had nothing left but two rooms of the house to live in. Eduard was arrested on trumped-up charges in the summer of 1939 and sent to a prison camp in December. They never saw him again.

In August 1941 mother-of-three Maria was summoned to the administrative centre in the nearest town, Kazulino. She took 10-year-old Leo with her, hoping to inspire mercy. But Leo returned alone. Fifty years later, Valy managed to find out that her mother was convicted of counter-revolutionary agitation and disappeared into the Gulag system on a 10-year sentence, which she did not survive. Valy became the head of the family at the age of 14 – three Swiss-Russian children, whose parents were enemies of the state, alone in a war zone. The children stayed on in the village, working in the collectivised farm and scavenging and begging for food as the war worsened around them. The village was alternatively occupied by German troops, deserters, partisans and Soviet troops and eventually burned to the ground by the Germans. In March 1943, Valy and her brothers made the decision to try to make their way to Switzerland. They joined neighbours and thousands of others who were fleeing west in the chaos of the war, passing through razed villages and muddy roads on an 18-day trek of more than 200 kilometres. When they reached the town of Vitebsk in Belarus, the Germans closed the roads and the orphans finally applied to the occupying army for help, seeking repatriation to Switzerland as Swiss citizens. They were billeted with a Russian family and had to wait for several months for Red Cross passes and train tickets to arrive. The children were sent to Berlin with German soldiers on a train journey of several days and nights. The Red Cross took charge of them in Berlin and an official accompanied them on the journey to Bern, where they had an uncle. He had emigrated to Switzerland as a young man. At 16, Valy was too old for school and was sent to work as a maid for a family. She was kindly treated and lived there for three years. Gradually she managed to pick up German. When she was old enough, she and her siblings petitioned the authorities for a small apartment so that they could live together but it wasn't to be. Valy trained as a milliner, and later had her own fur sewing business. Gennadi trained as a confectioner and Leo became a waiter. They spent the rest of their lives in Switzerland.

Valy recounted her life story to historian Carsten Goehrke and it appeared in a 2007 book about the Swiss diaspora in Russia *Die Besten Jahre Unseres Lebens* (The Best Years of Our Lives), by Peter Collmer. Gennadi is the only surviving sibling, living in Geneva. I asked him if he felt Swiss and he answered emphatically: "Yes, 200 per cent." He said he did his military service as a young man and would take up arms any time to defend Switzerland.

Many Swiss emigrants have held on to their nationality over the generations as a kind of insurance. Especially in politically unstable countries, you never knew when it might come in useful.

CHAPTER 4

The Swiss Are Brilliant

In the administration, and all through the whole of Switzerland – there are parties and continuous squabbles, pauperism, terrible mediocrity in everything. A workman here is not worth the little finger of a workman of ours. It is ridiculous to see and to hear it all. The customs are savage; oh, if you only knew what they consider good and bad here. Their inferiority of development: the drunkenness, the thieving, the paltry swindling that have become the rule in their commerce!

These are the words of the great Russian writer Dostoyevsky, from a letter written to a friend in the 1860s. He was living on the shores of Lake Geneva at the time, working on his novel *The Idiot*.

These days the Swiss are guilty of terrible excellence in everything, particularly science, industry and tennis. From Swiss 15-year-olds, who have the highest score outside Asia in mathematics in the Programme for International Student Assessment (PISA) rankings – and made the top 20 in science– to Swiss scientists and companies filing twice as many patents per capita as any other European country, high achievement has become the norm. Meanwhile, on the tennis court, the Swiss can bask in the glory of their most famous citizen, Roger Federer, who has earned a reputation for super-human talent and classy sportsmanship.

Switzerland is the sixteenth largest export economy in the world, and the second most complex economy, after Japan, according to the Economic Complexity Index (ECI). The Swiss have a knack for developing niche products, like dental implants and Nespresso coffee capsules. Between 2005 and 2015, the Swiss economy grew at 2.5% per year on average, outperforming all other western economies including the United States.

Swiss achievements are often played out on a grand scale. When the 57-kilometre Gotthard base tunnel opened in June 2016, it became the longest rail tunnel in the world, ahead of Japan's Seikan tunnel, and the Channel tunnel. The massive engineering project in the heart of the Swiss Alps took 17 years to complete, relying on the labour of 700 employees at any one time, who shifted a total of 28 million tonnes of rock. It was the third Gotthard tunnel to be built by the Swiss, but it won't be the last. In February 2016, voters gave the green light to the construction of a fourth Gotthard tunnel – and the second for cars.

Another international engineering marvel with a Swiss connection is the Large Hadron Collider, the largest machine and most complex experimental facility in the world. The particle collider at the European Organization for Nuclear Research (CERN) in Geneva is inside a 27-kilometre tunnel ring that runs under France and Switzerland. Built over 10 years, with the help of scientists and engineers from 100 countries, the collider is used to accelerate particles to almost the speed of light, so that scientists can smash them together and explore what matter is made of and what holds it together – in other words, to probe the fundamental structure of the universe. The presence of the collider has given a huge boost to Swiss research institutions, attracting the world's best minds in particle physics and other disciplines, and fuelled collaboration with leading universities worldwide. Thousands of CERN employees, fellows, associates and visiting scientists work from the labs and offices in Geneva every day, the place where the World Wide Web was invented by British scientist Tim Berners-Lee in 1989.

The list of scientific breakthroughs achieved by Swiss scientists is long and not always easy to explain in layman's terms. Among the more easily recognisable Swiss contributions to humanity are the first internal combustion engine used to power an automobile; the hallucinogenic drug LSD; artificial hip joints; the electric watch and electric toothbrush; the first effective flu medication, Tamiflu; and the Theory of Relativity, well known, if not well understood. Although several countries have a valid claim on Albert Einstein, in this instance he can safely be described as Swiss, as he was Swiss-educated, had become a Swiss citizen, and was still living and working in Switzerland when he developed his legendary theory.

$E=mc^2$

The Swiss have been accused of being too quick to claim certain high achievers with a foreign background as their own. Einstein is an example of Switzerland providing the right environment for an immigrant to reach his full potential. Einstein was a brilliant pupil but had problems performing in the regimented school system in Germany and did not attain a school-leaving certificate. At the age of 16, he came to Zurich to sit the entrance exam for the Zurich Polytechnic, later ETH Zurich. When he failed the exam, he was promised a place if he came back after completing his schooling. The young student flourished under the more progressive teaching ethos at an Aargau cantonal school and passed his Swiss Matura. He graduated from the Polytechnic in 1900 with a teaching diploma in maths and science.

While the other graduates from his year took up assistant lecturer posts at the Polytechnic Institute, Einstein was unable to secure a similar position there or elsewhere and started working as a private tutor. Before he completed his studies, he had applied for naturalisation and became a Swiss citizen in 1901. In a much-needed stroke of luck he finally managed to find the right job in 1902, as a technical expert in the Swiss Patents Office in Bern. He later wrote:

> Through this [finding a secure job], I was freed from the worry of making ends meet from 1902 to 1909, the years of my best productive work. Quite apart from that, the work on the definitive formulating of technical patents was a blessing for me. It made me think multilaterally, and also offered important stimulation for physical thought. Ultimately a practical job for people like me is a blessing. Because the academic career puts the young person under pressure to produce a large quantity of scientific papers – a temptation to resort to superficiality that only strong characters are able to withstand.

Life as a civil servant in Bern suited Einstein. There he married his university sweetheart Mileva Marić, and in 1904 their first son was born. The following year he obtained a doctorate from the University of Zurich and, in a burst of creativity, wrote five significant works on three areas of application – the reality and size of the atom, photons, and the Theory of Special Relativity. Einstein eventually held professorships at the two Zurich universities before leaving Switzerland for good in 1914.

Natural enemy

Einstein died in 1955, when Hans Rudolf Herren, the Swiss scientist who has arguably made the single greatest contribution to humanity in recent times, was just a little boy. Herren, recipient of the 1995 World Food Prize, and the Indiana Jones of entomology (the study of insects) was born and educated in

Switzerland. Another ETH Zurich graduate, Herren's hard work and innovation is credited with saving more than 20 million lives in Africa. At the centre of the drama was the tiny insect *Phenacoccus manihoti*, or mealybug, which was devastating the continent's cassava crop in the 1970s. Native to South America, cassava is a hardy plant grown by subsistence farmers across Africa. When Herren arrived at the International Institute of Tropical Agriculture in Nigeria in 1979, the crop was providing up to half of the daily nutritional needs of 200 million people. The sub-Saharan region was facing an unprecedented crisis: the mealybug, accidently introduced to Africa from South America, was spreading quickly from coast to coast, destroying four-fifths of the crop in some areas, raising the prospect of a humanitarian catastrophe.

In response, governments had embarked on a massive pesticide spraying programme, with the likelihood that ecosystems and other food supplies would be damaged. The mealybug was thriving because it had no natural predators in its new habitat, so Herren began to look for the right enemy to bring down the population naturally. Similar projects had succeeded elsewhere, but nobody had tried it on such a vast scale, from Senegal to Angola in the west and across the continent to the eastern island of Madagascar. Herren's approach to the problem showed a different kind of brilliance. After four years of painstaking detective work, Herren had identified a Paraguayan wasp that kills the mealybug but is harmless to other organisms. The next challenge was to find a way to introduce the wasp to its target in sufficient numbers. Herren helped raise USD 20 million from international institutions and governments and began a programme of ground releases coordinated with drops from planes.

It took time, but 13 years after Herren started working on the problem, mealybug numbers had stabilised to controllable levels in 30 countries. Africa's cassava reserves, and the people who depended on them, were saved.

Small is beautiful

Nanoscientist and analytical chemist Andreas Manz was working in Basel for the big Swiss chemicals firm Ciba-Geigy when disaster struck the city in 1986. A fire broke out on the night of 1 November in a storehouse for agrochemicals belonging to Ciba-Geigy's rival Sandoz, and by the time the blaze was brought under control, the fire-fighting water had flushed tonnes of toxic pesticides into the Rhine, turning the river red and decimating river life all the way to the North Sea. Driven by the desire to speed up the analysis of water samples, Manz went on to invent a new microlab chip technology that could analyse samples without the use of a laboratory. He figured out how to compress laboratory processes onto a card, or a microchip to be more precise, an innovation that would have a huge impact on medical and chemical analysis, reducing the testing time of fluids from weeks to seconds. Thanks to his work, it is now possible to conduct complex medical, biological or chemical analysis reliably and efficiently on microchips a few millimetres in size. The hybrid lab-on-a-chip technology has all sorts of applications, from glucose tests for diabetics to point-of-care diagnosis of diseases as diverse as malaria and HIV. Manz was honoured with a lifetime achievement award in 2015 by the European Patents Office. The Swiss researcher has clearly left his mark on microchip research. One essay of his on the concept of "miniaturised total chemical analysis systems", has been cited more than 11,000 times.

Swiss researchers produce roughly 1.2% of all scientific papers published worldwide, putting them in seventeenth place in international rankings, though the country is ninety-eighth in terms of population size. At 2.6 publications per 1,000 inhabitants, Swiss scientists are the world's most prolific publishers. The equivalent figures for the United Kingdom and the United States are 1.4 per 1,000 and .98 per 1,000 respectively. Along with Manz, Swiss chemistry Nobel Prize winners Richard R. Ernst (1991) and Kurt Wüthrich (2002) have helped bring up the average.

Sandoz merged with Ciba-Geigy in 1996 and formed Novartis, now the world's second-largest biotech and pharmaceutical company by revenue (after Johnson & Johnson), and one of Switzerland's great industrial success stories, with a market capitalisation of USD 280 billion, and 118,000 employees worldwide. Novartis' top-selling drugs include the cancer drug Gleevec / Glivec, blood pressure medication Diovan, and Ritalin for the treatment of ADHD.

Flying high

It takes more than gifted individuals to achieve great things, they also need a framework in which to thrive. In 2016, Switzerland topped the World Economic Forum's Global Competitiveness Index for the seventh consecutive year. The index rates competitiveness by allocating scores under 12 different "pillars". Switzerland leads the innovation pillar thanks to its world-class research institutions, high spending on research and development (R&D) by companies, and strong cooperation between the academic world and the private sector.

Because Switzerland's two national universities – the federal institutes of technology in Zurich und Lausanne – are renowned worldwide for their scientific output, they find it easy to attract foreign researchers and lecturers, with more than half of teaching staff in both institutes coming from outside Switzerland. It helps that Swiss university staff earn twice as much as they would in neighbouring countries. This has produced a "brain gain" to Switzerland's advantage.

Money also plays another role. Switzerland is among the countries with the highest spending on R&D in relation to gross domestic product. According to the State Secretariat for Education, Research and Innovation, the private sector bears the cost of over two-thirds of Swiss R&D expenditure, which currently amounts to nearly 3% of GDP, or around 16 billion francs. The Swiss National Science Foundation supports researchers in accessing long-term funding, saving them the headache of constantly having to chase grants.

The Solar Impulse project, a successful Swiss-led mission to fly a solar-power plane around the world, is an example of the close collaboration between the academic world and the private sector. The two experimental solar-powered planes of the Solar Impulse project captured the public imagination, in the quest to complete the first round-the-world flight without fuel. The project worked with industry partners and its scientific advisor, the Federal Institute of Technology in Lausanne (EPFL), to tackle the myriad technological challenges involved.

It is no surprise that the daring and ambitious project is the brainchild of a member of the Piccard family, famous in Switzerland and worldwide for their feats of innovation and adventure. Bertrand Piccard is one of the two men behind Solar Impulse. Alternating with André Borschberg, he flew different legs of the round-the-world route. Before being bitten by the solar-power bug, Bertrand Piccard set the record for the first non-stop balloon flight around the world. The record set by Bertrand's father Jacques in 1960 for descending more than 10,000 metres into the ocean depths in a purpose-built submersible or bathyscaphe still stands more than 50 years later.

The Solar Impulse aircraft is a lot more than an adventure challenge. The "flying laboratory" project is at the cutting edge of renewable energy technology and comes with a philosophy, according to the project website. "The record-breaking

Bertrand Piccard (left) and André Borschberg in Abu Dhabi where the round-the-world challenge started in March 2015

solo flight of five days and five nights without fuel [in July 2015] from Nagoya to Hawaii gives a clear message: everybody could use the same technologies on the ground to halve our world's energy consumption, save natural resources and improve our quality of life." After a nine-month gap in Hawaii to deal with technical problems, the plane took to the skies again in April 2016, and made good progress. Piccard finally landed back in Abu Dhabi after a total of 23 days of flight and more than 43,000 kilometres travelled.

When I visited two of the partner companies in Lausanne that contribute materials to the plane, I was struck by the extraordinarily specialised work that goes on behind the scenes. The fuselage frame, cabin and wings for the first prototype were made by Décision in collaboration with EPFL. It took a year to come up with a light enough material, a honeycomb carbon-fibre sandwich design that weighed 93 grams per square metre. By the time the second plane was being assembled by Décision, technicians and scientists had managed to produce carbon sheets weighing just 25 grams per square metre, the equivalent of six cubes of sugar.

Bértrand Cardis of Décision described the work as high tech but at the same time very artisanal. Some 6,000 hours of work went into each panel created for the fuselage. The technicians working on the aircraft have mostly been trained on-the-job from a young age under Switzerland's highly advanced apprenticeship system. This sort of technology transfer between science and industry is promoted in Switzerland and part of what makes the country an economic success and an interesting place to work.

This old house
High quality craftsmanship has a long tradition in Switzerland. If those activists from Uri, Schwyz and Unterwalden who signed the country's founding document, the Federal Charter, in 1291 wanted to go for a drink at a friend's house afterwards to celebrate, they could conceivably have visited the then-newly-built Bethlehem House in Schwyz.

I visited Bethlehem House for a swissinfo.ch report. Incredibly, this two-storey wooden house is still standing today, the oldest surviving wooden house in Europe. It is now a museum but was lived in continually until the 1960s. Constructed in 1287, it would not have taken as many hours to build as the fuselage panel of the Solar Impulse but would have required all hands on deck to complete the work in the months before winter set in again.

No one knows who the original occupants of Bethlehem House were, but they would have been people of standing in the community who earned their living from farming, as well as military service and administrative roles in the town. The Bethlehem folk would most likely have been supportive of their compatriots' bid for autonomy from the governors of the Counts of Habsburg.

Bethlehem House has always stood on this site. It was common practice in the Middle Ages and early modern times to dismantle houses and reassemble them on other sites because this was cheaper and quicker than building a new house

Bethlehem House may look like a simple farmhouse from the outside but it was only the well-to-do who could afford to build such a complicated and comfortable structure. The poor lived in much simpler shacks that have long since disappeared. The house, and the others of this vintage, were put together entirely with interlocking wooden beams. Not a single nail was used in the construction, as metal was too expensive in those days.

The longevity of Swiss vernacular architecture may not be attributable to brilliance alone. Bethlehem House escaped a fire in Schwyz in 1642 that destroyed 47 buildings in the town. So luck has played a part, but the Swiss values of taking the trouble to do a job well, and then taking proper care of one's possessions, must have improved its chances.

Pressure cooker

Does this culture of brilliance have a downside? There is an inevitable cost to the individual and to the environment, not always visible to the naked eye. A 2014 University of Bern study found that one quarter of the Swiss workforce felt exhausted and worn out. The representative study commissioned by Swiss Health Promotion found that some 300,000 people, or 6% of workers, were close to total burnout brought on by emotional, mental and physical exhaustion. The symptoms of burnout syndrome include chronic tiredness, loss of sleep and appetite, dizziness, pain, irritability, a sense of emptiness and unease, difficulties in concentration, and social withdrawal. Not exactly brilliant.

The pressure for perfection is also being felt by young children. By some estimates, half of all school-going children are receiving some sort of therapy to overcome learning difficulties at school. Two Swiss paediatricians, Thomas Baumann and Romedius Alber, were so concerned about the problem they wrote a book for professionals working with children, in an effort to combat the trend of over-diagnosis.

In an interview with the *Neue Zürcher Zeitung* newspaper, Alber, who is also a child psychiatrist, said children were being much more closely observed than in the recent past, and many deviations from the norm were being classed as developmental disorders, creating a massive therapy market.

"A huge number of school children are receiving special needs support at the wishes of their parents or because of societal pressure. You have psychomotor therapy and mathematical learning disorder therapy, dyslexia therapy and occupational therapy. On top of that, many parents bring their children to various alternative therapies. There is no end to it."

The pressure to meet high standards is also being felt by teachers, disproportionately compared to other professions.

One third of teachers were in serious danger of burnout, according to a 2014 study by the University of Applied Sciences Northwest Switzerland.

Switzerland's economic success has brought high population growth driven by immigration in the past few decades. Over the same period the fertility rate has remained low at 1.5 children per woman, perhaps another indication that people are under pressure. Since 2007, the average population growth rate has been above 1%, making Switzerland one of Europe's fastest growing countries by population. The permanent resident population is now 8.2 million and growing at around 100,000 per year. The latest projections from the Federal Statistics Office indicate that the Swiss population will reach nine million by 2023, much sooner than previously thought.

Not everyone is happy about this. An environmental organisation, Ecopop, made an unsuccessful attempt to curb population growth through a popular initiative in 2014. Though the backers tried to distance themselves from anti-foreigner sentiment, the initiative proposed imposing a limit of 0.2% net population growth per year, which would have meant a cap of 17,000 new immigrants coming into the country per year. The radical proposal was roundly rejected by three quarters of voters, although voters had accepted a less drastic initiative earlier the same year to restrict EU immigration by reinstating quotas, effectively taking the wind out of Ecopop's sails. The quotas require more negotiation with the EU and have yet to be enforced, so it remains to be seen what effect they will have.

A high standard of living and a fast-growing population inevitably has an impact on the environment, especially in a mountainous country where settlement is concentrated in one third of the national territory. Consumption by Swiss residents is exceeding the level that can be sustained by nature, particularly when the global impact is taken into account. Swiss residents produce around 700kg of municipal waste a year per head, half of which is recycled and half of which is incinerated. While the recycling rate is exemplary and the incineration is done relatively cleanly, the problem is that people are consuming too much. According to the 2015 Environment Report, if all countries were to use as many resources as Switzerland, around 2.8 Earths would be needed to meet the resulting demand. "Due to its patterns of economic and consumption activity, Switzerland is contributing more and more to the overexploitation of natural resources and ecosystems, not only at home but also abroad."

Paradise lost

Swiss Tourism promotes the image of a rural paradise dotted with charming historic towns and villages. An itinerary like this can still be found in Switzerland if you pick your route carefully, but the reality for many Swiss residents, especially those who can't afford to live in a prime location, is apartment-living in noisy and densely-populated areas. The report says an estimated 1.6 million people, or one in five inhabitants, are exposed to harmful and disturbing road traffic noise during the day; this falls only to one in six at night. Although stories about fussy Swiss people being disturbed by cow bells or church bells get media attention, road traffic is by far the most important and damaging source of noise.

Noise pollution goes hand-in-hand with air pollution. Despite significant improvement over the past 25 years, pollution from respirable particulate matter (PM10), ozone (O_3) and nitrogen oxides (NO_X) continues to exceed the legally prescribed ambient limit values, according to the Federal Office for the Environment. "Some 2,000–3,000 people still die prematurely every year due to air pollution, and the associated health costs are estimated at over CHF 4 billion per year. These costs are generated by diseases of the cardiovascular and respiratory systems and by cancer."

The loss of fertile land through the construction of built-up areas, leisure facilities, roads, and other infrastructure has been a creeping blight in Switzerland for decades, the environment report states, and the ongoing construction boom shows no signs of abating. At least eight football pitches of productive agricultural land is lost every day to construction, the impact made worse by poor spatial planning. With the remaining agricultural land Switzerland is not able to feed its own population but is still producing half of all plant foodstuffs and three quarters of animal foodstuffs consumed nationally – quite high considering the scant arable land available. The fertilisers and plant protection measures required to achieve this level of productivity are causing soil and water pollution.

The loss of meadows, pastures and wetlands has had a serious impact on biodiversity: one in three (36%) native species of animal, plant, lichen and fungus is now endangered, considerably higher than the average for OECD countries. Switzerland has failed to meet its own and international biodiversity targets.

It's not that the Swiss are not trying to do right by their environment. Progress has been made on air pollution, and water quality is generally good thanks to investment in water treatment plants. On an official level, the alarm has been sounded, and all the right commitments and strategies are in place. It is just notoriously difficult to deliver on environmental promises with so many competing interests making demands on natural resources. Switzerland is a very big ship to turn around.

Nobody does it better
Because of the Swiss reputation for quality, the designation "Swiss made" has become a valuable asset, and the debate on how to define and defend that asset has taken up a decade of airtime in the political system. Like an anaconda, the Swiss parliament takes a long time to digest meaty issues. In 2006, the government pro-

duced a report on the national brand in response to two parliamentary motions. The legislation that grew out of that report finally enters into force in 2017. It proved difficult to come up with a formula that would satisfy all the different sectors of the economy.

When it came down to deciding how Swiss a product has to be to claim the label "Made in Switzerland", the new law sets the bar relatively high. For industrial products, 60% of their value must originate in Switzerland. For food products, the share of Swiss raw material rises to 80% and for agricultural produce, including milk, the requirement is 100% sourced in Switzerland.

The label is important because consumers are willing to pay more if they know a product is Swiss. According to a St Gallen University study on the international perception of the Swiss brand, the added value of typical Swiss products and agricultural produce was 20% of the sales price. This went up to 50% for watches and luxury items. The Swiss watch industry has the most to lose from fraudulent Swiss branding. The fine watchmaking foundation, *Fondation de la Haute Horlogerie*, estimates 40 million fake Swiss watches are manufactured and sold worldwide ever year. The battle against counterfeiters is one of the main activities of the foundation in tandem with the Federation of the Swiss Watch Industry.

What is it exactly that consumers are willing to pay a premium for? The 2006 government report on the national brand defined Swiss *je ne sais quoi* in glowing terms. It's not the whole story but it's a story that sells well.

> For Swiss consumers as well as for foreign consumers, the concept of being Swiss (Swissness) generally means first and foremost a connection to an idyllic, well-ordered and efficient world. Swissness also encompasses terms such as precision, exactness, reliability and thoroughness. In the eyes of consumers, who associate numerous qualities with

Swiss products and services, Swissness also means top quality, and is in this sense a synonym for innovation, exclusive exports and outstanding services.

In a word, brilliant.

In focus: Victorinox

One of the most iconic Swiss products is the Swiss Army Knife produced by Victorinox. Not all Swiss companies are like Victorinox but most would like to be. The company, which grew from a cutler's workshop founded in 1884, is now led by Carl Elsener, the fourth generation of the Elsener family to do so. Its headquarters and the original factory are located in Ibach-Schwyz, less than one kilometre from Bethlehem House. More than 400 million Victorinox knives are already in drawers and pockets all over the world, and another 20 million are sold every year. The independent Swiss family company has a presence in over 130 countries, a global workforce of 2,000, and sells other categories of products including household and professional knives, watches, travel gear, clothing, and fragrances.

Although the original Victorinox Swiss officer's and sports knife was patented in 1897, around Einstein's time, the brand name "Swiss Army" originates in the United States, where it was established in the 1950s. The term "Swiss Army Knives" was created by American soldiers stationed in Europe during and after the Second World War who were impressed by the precision of the pocket knives used by the Swiss army and brought them home in large quantities as souvenirs. In 1950, Victorinox's American distributor Forschner Group started to market Victorinox pocket knives under the label "Swiss Army Knives". Victorinox took over both Forschner Group and the Swiss Army Knives brand in 2002. "We thought it important to own the

The iconic brand has retained its appeal for generations

name because it was created as a result of the qualities of the Swiss army's knife and, also, because it stands for all Victorinox products, especially in the North-American market," Elsener explained in an interview with *Competence* magazine.

There are 20 people working in the Victorinox R&D department, continually developing new products and updating existing ones. Elsener tells a story of how Swiss innovation works in other ways, beyond product development.

Pocket knives used to be a standard item in airport shops, but after the terror attacks of 9/11, the sale of knives was banned in duty free shops and in-flight, which resulted in a sharp fall of 30% in sales of Victorinox knives. "In order to avoid lay-offs, we went looking for firms in the region which temporarily needed extra staff, and lent them up to 80 of our employees for a period of four to eight months. This enabled us to survive a critical period in the history of our company without having to make anyone redundant," Elsener recalled.

Victorinox is a recipient of the Swiss Fairness Prize, in recognition for its record in personnel management. It also received an award from the Swiss Environmental Foundation. Waste heat from production processes is used to heat the production sites in Ibach-Schwyz and 120 homes nearby. In describing the typical Swiss attributes that have come to represent the Swiss brand, Elsener listed the usual positive characteristics of reliability, a strong work ethic, and a keen sense of quality, but he also added something more unexpected to the mix – humility.

CHAPTER 5

The Swiss Are Sexist

Here is one record the Swiss would like to forget: Switzerland was the last non-Arab country in the world to grant women full voting rights.

While the rest of the global community, near and far, gradually extended voting rights to women, beginning with New Zealand in 1893, Swiss men hogged the ballot box throughout a sixty-year domestic campaign for women's suffrage, until 1971. It was the ultimate silencing in a political system based on the voice of the people.

In Switzerland it was personal. Because of the direct democracy system, the battle could not be won in the courts or in parliament, but only in the hearts and minds of the men with whom Swiss women shared their lives and their country. Finally, on 7 February 1971, by a two-thirds majority, Swiss men accepted that Swiss women should have the right to vote at federal level. Some cantons and communes had already taken the step of extending voting rights, leading the way. Others were less progressive. The male voters of one canton, Appenzell Innerrhoden, refused to grant women the right to vote at cantonal level until forced to comply by a Federal Court ruling in 1990, a shameful delay that blighted the country's reputation for years to come.

Bear in mind that Switzerland is a country where there is a vote on every imaginable topic, from the treatment of drug addiction to the right to construct places of worship. The tiny canton of Appenzell Innerrhoden aside, 1971 was a different era. Times have changed. What relevance does the withholding of female suffrage have today?

Plenty, in fact. The people running the country today either came of age in a male-only political system or they were brought up by people who lived in that reality. Even the defence minister Ueli Maurer thinks nothing of making a sexist joke. During the unsuccessful 2014 campaign to convince voters to approve a three-billion-franc deal to replace thirty-year-old military jets, he told the same joke to four separate audiences: "How many used household appliances do you have at home more than thirty years old? At our place we don't have many, except of course the wife who does the housework."

But does this history of sexism have any real influence on women's position in Switzerland today? While there are slightly more female than male graduates emerging from Swiss universities and other higher level institutions today, when you look at the broader picture, Swiss women have historically benefitted much less from higher education than men. Just 34.4% of women between the ages of 25 and 64 have a tertiary qualification compared to 45.9% of men of the same age.

Tertiary education is heavily subsidised in Switzerland, with annual university fees ranging from only 1,000 francs to 4,000 francs. The men living in Switzerland today have enjoyed a greater share of this investment of public money and the advantages that come with it.

Perhaps women have benefitted in other ways? Such as a federally-subsidised childcare system that allows women to combine paid work and family duties without cancelling out too much of their earnings? Unfortunately not. A recent survey of workplace gender equality in 28 OECD countries by the *Economist* ranked Switzerland third from the bottom on childcare costs. Swiss childcare costs consume 41.2% of the average wage. Incidentally, Britain and Ireland brought up the rear in this category.

Well then, Swiss women must be spoilt when it comes to maternity leave? Actually, no. Though they have exemplary pregnancy and post-partum care, they are entitled to a mere 14 weeks of paid maternity leave. Not only is this one of the shortest in Europe, it is also the most recently granted. Voters rejected statutory maternity leave three times before finally accepting the principle of state-funded leave in 2004.

Perhaps the excellent state schools, attended by 95% of children, are structured in such a way that eases the childcare burden for families with school-age children? Wrong again. Most Swiss schools close for two hours in the middle of the day, with the expectation that someone will be at home to cook and care for the children.

Given this background, is it any wonder that women are poorly represented at decision-making levels in the economy? Although 30% of managerial posts are held by women, they don't seem to progress to the next level. Women occupy just 13.2% of positions in the boards of Swiss companies, against an OECD average of 20%.

Before you ask, women in Switzerland earn 25% less than men. Arguably the only perk enjoyed by Swiss women in the workforce is that they can retire one year earlier than their male colleagues, at 64. It's a pity this perk, which will be phased out by 2021, stems from an inherently sexist view of female capability.

Gender-based violence is also a problem in Switzerland, but the perpetrators and victims are 4.5 times more likely to be foreign nationals. Every two weeks a woman is killed at the hands of an intimate partner. A greater number survive attempted murder, while more than 3,000 suffer physical injuries.

The 17,685 reported incidents of domestic violence that took place in 2016 account for 38% of all violent crime. The perpetrators are male in the overwhelming majority of cases. There are 299 beds available in 18 women's shelters in Switzerland but a 2015 report by the cantonal directors for social policy *(Sozialdirektorenkonferenz)* found that 500 more places were needed to cater for women and children who are being turned away from shelters. There are two shelters operating for male victims of domestic violence.

The Swiss have a no-big-deal attitude to prostitution, probably because it has been a legal activity since 1942. Prostitutes have to register with cantonal and/or municipal authorities, abide by regulations, and pay tax and social insurance contributions on their earnings. In 2014, Zurich received massive international media coverage for its sex boxes (drive-thru brothels), an initiative to get sex workers off the streets that was hailed as a success by the city police after a two-year trial.

Until very recently, the country was known for its underage prostitutes, because the legal age to engage in prostitution was the same as the age of consent – 16. The legal age for a person to engage in prostitution was only raised from 16 to 18 in 2013 to comply with the European Convention for the Protection of Children against Sexual Exploitation and Sexual Abuse.

Behind the official position of treating prostitution as just another economic activity, Switzerland has a problem with forced prostitution and illegal prostitution, with a string of cases coming before the courts in recent years. FIZ, a Zurich NGO that cares for victims of trafficking, deals with around 100 new cases of migrant women in distress per year. A 2012 clampdown in the Italian-speaking canton of Ticino, "Operation Domino", led to the forced closure of 12 illegal brothels and the voluntary closure of 11 more. Where brothels are operating illegally, there is no way of protecting the rights or safety of the sex workers. More than half of the 170 women uncovered in the Ticino sting came from Romania, with others coming from Brazil, the Dominican Republic, Spain and Italy. In contrast, nearly all of the brothel owners or managers came from Canton Ticino.

In the legal sex industry, the Swiss offered special work permits to "cabaret dancers" from non-EU countries from 1995 to 2015. Under these permits, strip club owners could bring in foreign women for eight months at a time. In theory, the women were supposed to be free to choose whether to engage in prostitution on the side, but in practice it proved difficult to protect women from exploitation.

A long time coming

During the many votes on women's suffrage between the 1920s and 1970s, the argument in favour of keeping women out of the political process was twofold. On the one hand, the weaker sex had to be protected from the burden of the vote, and on the other hand, the work they were doing in the home was considered so important, nay sacred, that nothing could be allowed to interfere with it. A lot of emphasis was placed on how much women's (i.e. mothers') contribution to society in the home was cherished and respected. "Politicising" women would undermine this contribution, it was argued. Many women agreed. Nowadays no one would defend the exclusion of women from the political system, but Swiss society still places a high premium on women's role in keeping the home fires burning.

Although the right to vote was a long time coming, it was not for want of trying. The campaign for female suffrage made its first rallying cry when the Swiss Female Workers' Association called for votes for women in 1893. The Swiss Association for Women's Right to Vote was established in 1909 and the

Male voters rejected female suffrage by 70% in 1959

first test of public opinion came between 1919 and 1921 when male voters in six cantons rejected proposals to extend cantonal voting rights to women. At the Swiss Expo for Women's Work in 1928, activists paraded with a giant model of a snail on a float with the banner "Progress of Women's Right to Vote in Switzerland". Little did they know the vote was still a lifetime away.

The campaign posters give a fascinating snapshot of the emotional strings that were being pulled. Women's vulnerability was a big theme, with one image from the 1959 vote on female suffrage depicting a woman and child recoiling in fear as a giant menacing hand reaches for them under the caption "Protect her. A woman should not be prey to the parties." (See previous page)

Neglect of duty was another key topic, dramatised in one 1920 poster by an image of a smashed-up household and a distressed infant on the floor with the caption "The mother is practising politics."

To find out more about the struggle for female suffrage, I went to visit one of the last surviving leaders of the suffrage movement, 98-year-old Marthe Gosteli. The veteran campaigner welcomed me at the archive of the Swiss women's rights movement she founded on the outskirts of Bern. The Gosteli Archive spans more than a century of activism and it is housed in her original family home. In her lifetime, Marthe Gosteli has witnessed the social and economic transformation of her country. The pretty old country house in Worblaufen that was once the centre of a large landholding of rolling fields is now swamped by decades of development: railway lines, motorways and housing encroach on all sides.

In her capacity as vice president of the national umbrella body for women's associations, *Bund Schweizerischer Frauenorganisationen*, and chair of its working group for political rights, Gosteli negotiated with the government in the lead-up to the 1971 vote. During the previous vote on extending the right to vote to women in 1959, Gosteli was a member of the executive committee of the Bern association.

Marthe Gosteli (1917–2017) was one of the last surviving Swiss suffragettes

Today Gosteli looks like the proverbial little old lady. She walks with the aid of two sticks but the intensity of her personality is undiminished, and she demands sharp eye contact when making a point. Ironically, she explained, it was the pronounced democratic and federal structure of Swiss democracy that hampered progress towards full democracy. Gosteli and her colleagues were fighting a battle on dozens of fronts: "Many people don't understand why it took so long. We had to win on three levels – communal, cantonal and federal. Full political collaboration was only possible when we had the right to vote on all three."

Her only complaint now is that the achievement of female suffrage has lost recognition. "Huge work was done by many brilliant women in our country and no-one knows about it."

As recently as 2013, Swiss national television and radio ran a history series about the great Swiss who had shaped the nation. The series focused on the founding days of the Swiss Confederation and the nineteenth century, and all six historical figures selected were men. When the episodes aired, the national broadcaster invited the public to take part in a debate about Swiss identity. Inevitably the question came up about the absence of women, and the Swiss Broadcasting Corporation gave this explanation:

"The restriction to certain epochs in the past has had the result that women are absent – at least as leading figures. This can be explained by the circumstances of those times, in which visible politics was decided by men." Maybe if there is a second twentieth century edition of the history series, Marthe Gosteli and her fellow campaigners might get the recognition they deserve.

Massive societal change was needed for women and men to recognise the full potential of women. There was even a counter movement of women's organisations objecting to the political goals of Gosteli and her colleagues, and actively fighting against them.

"We believed the most important thing was to give women the opportunity to get an education or train for a profession. If they were independent and earned their own money, it would change the mentality and people would realise what women were capable of," Gosteli said. She herself worked for the Swiss army press and radio division during the Second World War and later for the American Embassy information service. The veterans of the women's movement can take pride in the fact that Switzerland now has one of the highest rates of female participation in the workforce, at 77%.

The 40-year commemorations have come and gone but some norms relating to gender roles still hold firm, as is seen in the work-family arrangements negotiated between couples (only 16% of mothers with children aged under 25 are employed full-time) and in divorce laws, which enshrine a stay-at-home mother's right not to work outside the home until her youngest child is 10. There is also the retirement age anomaly, allowing women to retire one year earlier than men at 64, despite the fact that women have a longer life expectancy.

There were other indignities Swiss women had to put up with in the relatively recent past, including losing their citizenship upon marrying a foreigner (up to 1992), or losing control of their assets upon marriage (up to 1988). Rape within marriage was made a prosecutable offence in 1992 but only became a crime in 2004. The worst fate was saved for unmarried pregnant women up to the 1970s, who faced internment for "licentiousness", and the forced adoption of their children. Forced sterilisation was also a Swiss phenomenon, continuing in rare cases up to the 1980s and predominantly inflicted on women. In a 2005 paper on eugenics, Regina Wecker of the University of Basel explained how vulnerable women were put under pressure. "Patients' files at the Psychiatric Clinic and the Psychiatric Polyclinic in Basel show that women were pressured by, e.g. making their release from the Psychiatric Clinic or an *Arbeitserziehungsanstalt* ['work-house'] contingent on their agreeing to a sterilisation. Or an abortion was only granted if a woman gave her consent to sterilisation." Wecker found other documents that showed the authorities threatened to withdraw financial help. In 2011, *Beobachter* magazine reported on the case of Bernadette Gächter, a pregnant 18-year-old psychiatric patient in 1972, who was labelled "psychopathic" and put under severe pressure to agree to an abortion and sterilisation. The same doctor had also sterilised Gächter's mother earlier in his career. But these tragic stories belong to a different era and are sadly not unique to Switzerland.

The Swiss delay in granting women the vote, and the late introduction of other key rights and entitlements, such as gender equality in marriage and even maternity leave, have earned the country a reputation for being behind the times on women's rights. But does this assessment stand up to closer scrutiny?

Women in politics

Let's start at the top with a roll-call of presidents this decade. 2010: Doris Leuthard (female); 2011: Micheline Calmy-Rey (female); 2012: Eveline Widmer-Schlumpf (female); 2013: Ueli Maurer (male); 2014: Didier Burkhalter (male); 2015: Simonetta Sommaruga (female); 2016: Johann Schneider-Ammann (male).

Four out of seven is impressive. The presidency in Switzerland is a largely ceremonial role rotating on a one-year basis between the seven members of the Federal Council. The president continues to look after his or her portfolio alongside presidential duties. Nevertheless, it's obviously a very important and visible job, and when the cabinet includes women ministers who stick around for long enough, they step into the role. In 2011, when the number of female ministers outnumbered the number of men in cabinet for the first time ever, the news made international headlines. This is a country which saw its first female minister, Elizabeth Kopp, in 1984, and first woman president, Ruth Dreifuss, in 1999. Dreifuss represented another first for Switzerland, being the country's first Jewish president.

At the time of writing there were two female ministers out of seven, which is a more accurate reflection of the power-sharing breakdown at parliamentary and cantonal level, where women are still outnumbered two or three to one. In the 2015 federal parliamentary elections one third of the candidates were women, and almost 29% (compared to 43% in Sweden, and 20% in the US) of those elected to the two houses of parliament were female (although just 15% of seats in the 53-seat Senate went to women). This implies that there is no reluctance to elect women. Despite this progress, the adversarial nature of politics is still discouraging many women from throwing their hat into the ring. When I spoke to the organiser of a preparation course for women interested in getting into politics, she said part of the problem was that women didn't identify strongly enough with a particular party to want to defend their whole platform. The women who attended the course also needed help with confidence and communication skills. These factors are obviously not unique to Switzerland.

The cut and thrust of politics can put some women off, but luckily not all. In a 2015 interview with *Annabelle* magazine, then Swiss President Simonetta Sommaruga described how she had reacted in her early days as a consumer rights advocate taking part in debates. "One time I was so destroyed [*fertiggemacht*] by an opponent that I burst into tears afterwards and swore I would never leave myself so exposed again." After that she practised similar debates with her husband, the writer Lukas Hartmann, to build up her confrontation skills.

Women and work
Only half of the 25% gap in salary between men and women can be explained by factors such as qualification level. The two sectors where women are most severely discriminated against are two of the country's most successful – finance and the chemical industry. Patricia Widmer, now head of the English-speaking "Women Back to Business" programme at the University of St Gallen, experienced first-hand the limitations imposed on women in the banking sector.

"My career had taken a very traditional path. I studied business and economics at University of Zurich and graduated with an MBA in Banking and Finance like so many other people in Switzerland. Then I went to work for UBS where I was a relationship manager. Everything went smoothly. It was while I was working for a private bank that I became pregnant with my first child in 2004. No woman in this bank had ever come back to work after maternity leave, not one. I wanted to fight, I really wanted to be the first one to do that so I came up with a flexible working concept. My immediate boss actually agreed but his superior would not hear of it. We had a talk and he asked: 'Will you be able to live with the idea that everybody in your team has to work more just that you can have such an arrangement?' When he asked me that, I thought, OK, that's it, I can't work here any more."

Instead of looking for another job immediately, Widmer enrolled in further education. After several years abroad with her husband, living in the United States and Germany, Widmer returned to Switzerland, a mother-of-two. She attended the Women Back to Business course and managed to land the all-elusive prize – a rewarding part-time job with responsibility. But this time she experienced the other side of the double-edged sword, the general disapproval of women who choose to work rather than be at home for their children every day.

"The perception of a lot of people, even young people – and I'm always shocked about that – is why do you have to go to work as a woman? If you as a woman have to go to work, it means that the husband can't afford to keep the family."

Lack of affordable childcare is often singled out as an obstacle to having children in Switzerland. While it's true there are not enough day care places to meet the demand, day care is not the preferred choice for many Swiss parents. Handing your children over to the care of "strangers" – *fremdgeben* – still has a stigma attached to it in Swiss society. Remember, not that long ago, poor families and single parents were forced by the authorities to hand over their children into an inadequate care system. This was not only due to the tradition of "placing" poor children as indentured farm labourers, but also because, unlike in other countries, the welfare authorities in the communes with decision-making power were close to the individual cases. It was not so easy to slip through the net undetected. The communes appointed welfare committees who had local knowledge of the circumstances of families in need and the power to intervene. The model of the successful family with a father earning enough money and the mother looking after the children in an exemplary way had more than just respectability value. It was important for the family's ability to stay together.

It is difficult to believe that before 2005, Switzerland did not have statutory paid maternity leave. Voters rejected the outlandish notion that a woman be guaranteed paid time off after giving birth in 1974, 1984, 1987 and again in 1999. Oddly enough, the state was willing to use social contributions to pay for men to be absent from work for two to three weeks per year up to the age of 30 or older to complete their military service, the equivalent of two terms of maternity leave. And yet, every time maternity pay came to a vote, several parties campaigned vigorously against it. In the end, paid leave became law with only 55% of the vote.

Opponents claimed that most women were already enjoying comfortable working conditions, including, for many, paid maternity leave. Could employers not just be trusted to fund and look after this one themselves?

No they could not, voters eventually decided. As a result Swiss women are now entitled to 14 weeks' state subsidised maternity leave, which is still one of the shortest in Europe, but progress nonetheless. Unfortunately, time off for babies is still relegated to being a women's issue, and fathers are still waiting for paid paternity leave.

The lunch pickle
There is a sweet sight in Swiss towns and villages at around 11.30 in the morning when the children are let out of school.

You see them getting onto the public buses or walking home, the smallest ones wearing their regulation reflective triangles – another day in paradise. School is closed for the next two hours, and the children can eat a hot meal at home and relax before going out again, replenished, for the second half of their school day from 1.30pm to 3.30pm, in most cases.

What you don't see are the women in the kitchens, frantically putting away shopping while chopping and stirring, doing their bit to live up to the Swiss ideal of the family eating together in the middle of the day.

What would it do to your day if you had to guarantee a hot meal on the table for your children at 12pm, no matter where you were or what you were doing? That is the reality for most Swiss families. It is still not standard for schools to provide lunch and supervision on-site during the midday break. Those that do are known as *Tagesschule* (day schools), and in most cases, parents must pay for the extra services. In some cases, a separate entity offering lunch and after-school care has been set up where parents can apply for paid places. Where I live, a canton without day schools, this service is over-subscribed, with some parents not being able to find places for any of their children, or not all of their children, or not all the days they need. Where Patricia Widmer lives, the *Mittagstisch* (lunch table) is undersubscribed and people feel sorry for the children who have to go there because their mothers are not at home.

Many schools and communes have yet to introduce any infrastructure for this childcare gap, and they are under no obligation to do so. But the approach is changing, especially in more urban areas. Beginning in 2016, Zurich converted six schools to the full-day timetable with a hot meal provided on site, with a view to making this model compulsory from 2018. A study by Basel city's education department found that one in four primary school children were being provided with a meal

EMPLOYMENT SITUATION OF MOTHERS LIVING IN A HOUSEHOLD WITH A PARTNER AND CHILD(REN), 2015

By the age of the youngest child

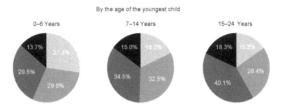

0–6 Years   7–14 Years   15–24 Years

EMPLOYMENT SITUATION OF MOTHERS LIVING ALONE IN A HOUSEHOLD WITH CHILD(REN), 2015

By the age of the youngest child

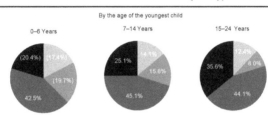

0–6 Years   7–14 Years   15–24 Years

EMPLOYMENT SITUATION OF FATHERS LIVING IN A HOUSEHOLD WITH A PARTNER AND CHILD(REN)

By the age of the youngest child

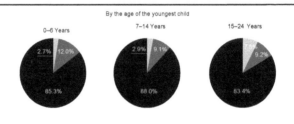

0–6 Years   7–14 Years   15–24 Years

Not in Paid Employment   Part-Time < 50%   Part-Time 50–89%   Full-Time 90–100%

Figures do not include the unemployed (as defined by the ILO)

Source : BFS – SAKE   © BFS, Neuchâtel 2016

and supervision during the lunch-time break, the availability of places having increased fourfold over 10 years. For mothers in the workforce, this means the conversation topic of where the children eat at midday never runs out of steam. If there are no organised options available, you might find a childminder close to the school who provides *Mittagstisch*, or arrange for your children to go to a classmate's home for lunch, or ask the grandparents to step in. Finding five solutions for Monday to Friday is a tall order. Is it any wonder the vast majority of working mothers of school-age children work part-time? In fact, the apron strings are so tight in Switzerland that the overwhelming majority of women with children under 25 work part-time at most. Fewer than one in five mothers living with a partner whose children are aged between 15 and 24 work full-time (18.8% to be exact), 17% don't have a paid job and a quarter work 50% or less. (See previous page)

For parents who have genuinely chosen to stay at home to be the primary carers of their children, Switzerland provides something of a safe haven. Their presence at home is accepted, rather than questioned as it would be in other industrialised countries, and is to a large extent indispensable. There are many parents who cherish the fact that their children can come home for lunch, and children who enjoy the respite and home cooking too. But this model carries the risk of creating a gilded cage where stay-at-home mothers can't see a way out. Their children may be away for 20 or 30 hours a week but the hours are broken up in such a way that it becomes devilishly complicated to think of taking on another commitment, paid or not.

Within Switzerland, one interesting exception to the home-for-lunch model is the Italian-speaking canton of Ticino, whose children have been attending full days of school or kindergarten (from age three) since the 1970s.

Things are complicated enough for two-parent families. The majority of social welfare recipients are households headed by one parent. How many more of them would be able to hold down a job if their children weren't coming and going every couple of hours? Bear in mind too that job seekers are expected to include their marital status and the dates of birth of their children on their CVs, information that is much more likely to weigh against female applicants.

At 1.5 children per woman, the fertility rate in Switzerland is low (close to the EU average of 1.59), and yet there have been no major public policy changes to encourage people to have more children. The real birth rate among Swiss women is lower (1.4) because foreign-born women are bringing up the average. There are proportionally more foreign-born women of childbearing age in Switzerland and they have more children than their Swiss counterparts (with a fertility rate of 1.8), starting at a younger age. The average age of maternity for Swiss women is 32; for foreign-born women it is 30. The outcome is that almost four out of 10 children in Switzerland are born to a foreign mother, double the rate that was seen in 1990, even though foreign women only make up 22% of the female population.

Part-time pinch

For *swissinfo.ch*, I did a series of interviews with women about work-life balance. I spoke to a full-time working mother of two who was full of praise for the *Tagesschule* that her children attended in Bern. Having her children in school for an uninterrupted day meant she and her husband only had the after-school hours to organise, and she felt full-time work was manageable. However, she said that other mothers were speechless when they realised that she worked full-time. At the other extreme, a mother-of-three I spoke to who had given up her job after the first baby was content with her arrangement too. She was glad her husband earned enough to support the family and he was glad that she, the children's mother, was doing all the childcare. The financial freedom to make this traditional choice, along with an enduring climate of approval for this model of family life, makes Switzerland a more comfortable place for stay-at-home mothers than many other industrialised societies.

One part-time worker I spoke to would have liked to work more hours, but only if her husband was able to reduce his hours and step in. She is one of a large number of women who are keen to increase their hours but are prevented from doing so either by workplace opposition or childcare logistics. Meanwhile the majority of men working full-time (nine out of 10 in one study) want to reduce their hours but either don't have the option to do so or they fear repercussions for their careers if they do make that choice. Given these obstacles, it is an encouraging sign that the rate of fathers working part-time in Switzerland is 10% and rising, which is opening up more opportunities for both parents.

Is the fact that most mothers work part-time a negative point when it comes to gender equality or have Swiss women found a happy medium in treading water in their careers while their children are young? Opinions differ, but it is significant that Swiss women rarely ramp up their hours to full-time when their children get older.

When mothers meet at the playground and the conversation turns to work, the question is never "What do you do?", it is, "What percentage do you work?" As if the "what" is no longer important because the game is lost anyway. Among the applicants for the Women Back to Business course, Patricia Widmer sees many women who want to achieve more on the professional side but have been blocked in some way, either by internal or external factors.

"Working mothers usually work a very low percentage, one to two days a week, and do lower qualified work in order to be able to work part-time. This means a lot of the women who studied at university either don't go back to work because they can't find a challenging job or they go into a low qualification job and get stuck. Once you have that on your CV it is really hard to get out of that level. It is almost the same as if you had stopped working altogether."

The net result is that women are still woefully under-represented at decision-making level in the business world. The mere 13% female share of board directors is also true across senior management. Swiss Federal Councillor Sommaruga has secured cabinet backing for her plans to introduce legislation to impose non-binding quotas for boards, which sounds like an oxymoron but would still force companies to pay attention to the problem. Parliament still has to approve the legislation which would require companies that fail to meet the target to explain themselves and outline plans to comply. This may make a difference in the future, but the real problem seems to be lower down the chain. As long as women are disappearing from the paths that lead to management, the culture in Swiss firms will not change.

The abortion barometer

There are other kinds of decisions that matter to women. A country's stance on abortion is a good barometer of attitudes towards women's sexuality and self-determination in that society. Switzerland was one of the first countries in Europe to legislate for abortion in 1937, though at the time, and for the next six decades, it allowed abortion only when the woman's health was in danger. The cantons were free to decide how strictly to interpret the law, which led to a patchwork of abortion services, with some cantons operating a liberal regime and others making it very difficult for women to access legal abortions in their hospitals. This caused women to travel from canton to canton inside the country for abortion, right up to 2002 when voters accepted the new abortion law allowing unrestricted access to abortion in the first trimester of pregnancy and setting the conditions under which abortions could be carried out in the second trimester.

There hasn't been much political mileage in the abortion issue until very recently when a group of campaigners collected enough signatures for a 2014 popular vote calling for abortion to be excluded from the list of procedures covered by the mandatory health insurance package. Every Swiss resident is obliged to take out this basic health insurance, the elements of which are defined by law. Above that basic package consumers are free to take out additional insurance for extra bells and whistles treatment. The proposal put forward by an inter-party group of mainly conservative Christians was entitled "Make abortion funding a private matter". The idea was that abortion, which raised moral questions, didn't belong in the category of regular health services, and that those who objected to abortion on principle shouldn't be forced to fund the procedure indirectly through their insurance premiums. It was suggested that women or girls who thought they might someday wish to have an abortion could take out an additional insurance policy to cover this eventuality. In February 2014, almost 80% of voters rejected the initiative, giving a clear indication of the level of acceptance of abortion as a women's health issue.

At 6.3 abortions per 1,000 women aged between 15 and 44, Switzerland has one of the world's lowest abortion rates, achieving the safe, legal and rare standard aspired to by women's reproductive rights advocates. This is a reflection of fewer unplanned pregnancies among Swiss women. Since 1981, a federal law on family planning centres has guaranteed free access to counselling and help in matters concerning pregnancy and family planning throughout Switzerland. With the advent of medical abortion, close to three-quarters of Swiss abortions are now non-surgical and take place within the first nine weeks of pregnancy.

The Swiss women I've spoken to, professionally and privately, who have had abortions are quite matter-of-fact about the experience. They fall into the majority category of women who have ended pregnancies for "psycho-social" reasons. But as is the case in any country I've spent time in, discussions between women about personal stories of abortion only ever take place on a one-to-one basis in confidence. It is not a dinner-party topic in Switzerland, any more than elsewhere.

A story of change

The story of women in Switzerland in living memory is a story of enormous change and progress. The woman of 1970 could not vote in a federal election or referendum. Without family support she would find it practically impossible to keep a child born "out of wedlock". The woman of 1987 lost control of her assets on marriage. The woman of 1991 lost her citizenship on marrying a foreigner (see "In focus", below) and could be raped by her husband without having recourse to the law. The Swiss woman of 1998 had never seen a female president. The woman of 2004 had no legal guarantee of receiving maternity pay. The woman of 2011 was effectively forced to take her husband's name on marriage, unless she had bagged one of the rare men who would agree to take his wife's name. Equal pay was enshrined in the Constitution in 1980, and if not fully achieved, is at least enforceable. Until the 1990s, military service secured huge networking advantages for men; officer rank was virtually a must for anyone with managerial ambitions. But even this seemingly impermeable rock of privilege has dissolved in the multicultural and open economy of today.

This steady morphing of women into the legal equivalent of male Swiss citizens has been hard won and is to be celebrated. The old separation between *Männersache* (men's affairs) and *Frauensache* (women's affairs) has worn thin, making it possible for women and men to expand their horizons in more fulfilling ways. Swiss women are confident, well-educated and active in their society. Despite problems in advancing on the career track, I believe a tipping point has been reached. Yes, it's true that rights won in comparable countries came much later to the Swiss, but this delay can now work to Switzerland's advantage, allowing Swiss society to cherry pick the best solutions to gender inequality and make more judicious choices about how best to reconcile the needs of its families and its economy.

In focus: Swiss wives club

Four in ten Swiss brides and grooms choose a foreign spouse, who may apply for naturalisation after five years of marriage. The presence of these new Swiss, bringing in different ideas and norms, has had a dynamic effect on a micro level, within families, and on a broader societal level. Until relatively recently (1992), a foreign woman automatically became Swiss upon marriage to a Swiss man. This shortcut did not apply to foreign men who married Swiss women. In that case the Swiss women lost their Swiss citizenship and their children did not count as Swiss. Under this unequal system, Switzerland lost many of its own female citizens and gained brand new ones. Marijka Moser is one such naturalised Swiss wife.

Moser is a Swiss grandmother who does not fit any stereotype that might be conjured up by that description. Because her pension is small, she works as a lunchtime pizza courier five days a week. She lives in a converted camper van on the outskirts of Solothurn with a dog and four cats. Since she moved

Marijka Moser at her home in Solothurn

in 10 years ago, more people have come, and there are now eight wagons in the settlement, clustered around a dilapidated main building that used to house migrant workers.

Moser first came to Switzerland from the Netherlands in 1971 at the age of 22. Her Swiss boyfriend, Albrecht Moser, had organised a three-month work permit, and when the three months were up, the police knocked on the door reminding her to leave. Before long the couple decided to get married and a year later, Marijka returned, this time as a Swiss citizen through marriage. The couple shared a passion for long-distance competitive running. Within three weeks she was wearing the national colours of Switzerland at the European Championships in Paris. At that time, the prevailing opinion in athletics and medicine was that women's bodies were not suited to long-distance running. The longest race a woman could run in official competitions was 800m. But times were changing.

"I was born 10 years too soon. The longer the distance, the better for me. They introduced the 1,500m but even that was too short for me. My husband qualified for the Munich Olympics so I improved my time on the 1,500 and qualified too. The following year they introduced the 3,000." Moser and her husband, who have since divorced, shared a live-in job as school caretakers and scraped together a living. Their travel and sportswear was paid as national competitors but nothing else. On a free day they would go for a two-hour run together. Albrecht was preparing for the Morat-Fribourg road race.

The Morat-Fribourg race had become popular in its 40 years in existence. The 18-km race is held every October to commemorate a legendary journey made by a soldier who brought the news of victory from Morat to Fribourg at the end of the Battle of Morat in 1476. Albrecht Moser had taken part in the race eight times, and even come in second. Marijka used to go along to watch him compete in various races, but on the day of the Morat-Fribourg race in 1973 she didn't feel like watching from the side lines any more.

"I decided very spontaneously. Why not me? I thought. My husband was getting ready for the race that morning and I grabbed a spare number that was lying around. It wasn't even for that race. I didn't sign up or anything. I just tied my hair back, pinned the number on me to blend in and went along to the start of the race. One of the organisers spotted me. He was running too. 'You shouldn't do this,' he said. 'This is disrespectful.' But I told him to speak with me later. So I ran the race. The other runners were so kind to me, smiling and giving me glucose sweets. I was fit, and I ran a good race. I got so close to the finish I could see the finish line but two stewards grabbed me and pulled me out of the race."

After braving the hostility of the organisers, Moser received positive reactions to her ground-breaking decision to attempt the race. Her life didn't change, but she became "*la femme de Morat-Fribourg*". Four years later women were finally allowed to compete in the race. These days, when not working or spending time with family, Moser pursues her passion for endurance riding events and travels around on horse-related trips. Does she think of herself as Swiss? "I see myself as a European really but yes, my heart did beat faster when I saw the Swiss flag at running events."

CHAPTER 6

The Swiss Are Neutral

For hundreds of years, Swiss blood was spilt fighting in wars for foreign kings and emperors all over Europe. Mercenary was a respectable Swiss profession, and Swiss soldiers were known as some of the best that could be hired. But today, after two centuries of unbroken neutrality, the Swiss are famous for not fighting in any wars. The warriors have become pacifists? Not so fast: the Swiss still have a special interest in international conflicts, and military activity is big business both at home and abroad.

Swiss neutrality as we know it today owes its existence to two important historic landmarks – the French Revolution of 1789 and the Congress of Vienna in 1815 – and the events that happened between these dates.

Blood for Money

Though the Swiss hadn't fought a battle in their own name on foreign soil since 1515, Swiss hired-swords enjoyed a solid reputation all over Europe from the Middle Ages up to the mid-nineteenth century for their loyalty and fighting prowess. In return for protection or money, the Swiss cantons provided men to European monarchs to fight in wars or serve as palace guards and bodyguards. This service abroad was a way for Swiss men to make some money and see the world – the only downside being great personal risk.

The French kings loved the Swiss the most, maintaining 11 infantry regiments and a royal guard of more than a thousand men in the eighteenth century, and it was this relationship that cost the Swiss troops the greatest single loss of life in modern times. The fateful date was 10 August 1792, the day the French monarchy fell.

Three years had passed since the Revolution but a 950-man strong Swiss Guard still protected the Tuileries Palace in Paris, where Louis XVI and his much-maligned wife were detained with their two children. In her highly-respected biography of Marie Antoinette, Antonia Fraser writes about the Swiss:

> The Cent-Suisses du Roi constituted an impressive body of crack troops. They led somewhat segregated lives in their barracks, preserving their own language and customs, although they had been in the service of the French king since the late fifteenth century and had a French colonel-in-chief, the Duc de Brisac. On ceremonial occasions, they still wore the ancient uniform of the liberators of Switzerland, but were otherwise dressed in blue uniforms braided in gold, with red breeches.

On the morning of 10 August 1792, fearing imminent attack, the royal family left their residence in the Tuileries and walked across the gardens to the adjoining National Assembly, and ultimately to their doom. Left with no clear instructions, and hopelessly outnumbered by the forces and mob massing outside, the Swiss were massacred:

> And so began the killings, which left the Tuileries a shambles of blood, corpses, severed limbs, broken furniture and bottles. People were hurled out of windows, killed in cellars, stables and attics, and even in the chapel where some

had sought sanctuary, pleading vainly that they had not fired their guns. ... Many of those who tried to flee, whether Swiss or courtiers, were cut down by the mounted gendarmerie in the Place Louis XV. Paris became one huge abattoir, its gutters filled with the corpses of the Swiss, stripped naked and often mutilated. Traumatised wayfarers saw men kneeling in the streets and pleading for mercy before being beaten to death.

An estimated 600 Swiss Guards were killed in the fighting or massacred after surrender, 60 were taken prisoner and killed by the crowd, and a further 160 died of their wounds in prison. Fewer than 100 of the 950 Swiss men serving in the Tuileries that day are known to have survived.

Adding insult to injury

It would get worse. France invaded in 1798, nabbing the Swiss heartlands – and Bern's treasury – in order to pursue war against Austria. In 1799, thanks to Napoleon's activities, the new Helvetic Republic was invaded by the Russians and Austrians and became the theatre of a European war. This pattern would continue for more than a decade. When the French left in 1802, the new Republic collapsed amid anarchy and civil war. Napoleon reasserted control, only to have Austrian troops cross Swiss borders again in December 1813. But the Swiss would have their day: when the dust finally settled after the demise of the French emperor's dreams of European domination, the Congress of Vienna gave the Swiss not only the new cantons of Neuchâtel and Valais, but also recognized the perpetual neutrality of the country.

The Congress of Vienna was a historic opportunity for the Swiss, whose desire for neutrality fit the new formula for stability in Europe. It also united the nation. (There was just one more obstacle to overcome – the old religious division that had plagued the country since the Reformation. A brief civil war was needed before the modern Swiss state, Confoederatio Helvetica, was founded in 1848.)

Mercenary units were banned by the new Swiss Constitution of 1848 and it became illegal for Swiss men to fight in foreign armies in 1859, officially putting an end to a centuries-long tradition. Unofficially, the Swiss continued to enlist abroad, some unable to resist the lure of military adventure or the call of duty to defend weaker countries. Thousands fought in the First World War, mainly on the French side, and the Swiss joined the French Foreign Legion in significant numbers. Some 400 Swiss were found guilty of breaking the law against foreign military action between 1936 and 1939 when they went off to fight on both sides in the Spanish Civil War. In the Second World War, Swiss men who joined the Free French Army under de Gaulle also faced jail on their return to Switzerland. An overwhelming majority strongly opposed Nazism, which represented the enemy at the gates, but there were cases of Swiss fighters joining the Nazi cause. And in the twenty-first century, according to the Swiss Federal Intelligence Service, there have been 73 known cases of people leaving Switzerland to fight in jihadist conflicts – though not all for the same groups. The first of a handful of people to be prosecuted for fighting in Syria or for connections to Islamic State was a man who joined the terror group in December 2013 and returned after a few weeks, regretting his actions. In lieu of a prison sentence, the young man was given 600 hours of community service and fined. He was also required to attend counselling and complete a photographic project on the theme of peace.

Military might
Seventy years after the end of the Second World War, Switzerland is the only country in Western Europe where air raid si-

rens can still be heard regularly. A network of 7,800 sirens covers the entire country, and they are tested once a year, on the first Wednesday in February. Even if I've heard the radio announcements or seen the reminder in the newspaper, that haunting ascending and descending sound, familiar from news reels and war movies, fills me with a feeling of trepidation. I should be reassured by the fact that there are nuclear shelters under most residential buildings for use in the case of armed conflict or disasters, but I'm not.

Another disconcerting experience is coming face to face with large groups of armed troops on public transport. On the two or three annual call-up days for new recruits, young men from all over Switzerland abandon their jobs, apprenticeships or studies and make their way to army barracks for several months of live-in training. The recruits can also be seen in large numbers on their way to or from weekend leave. The presence of so many soldiers on the move creates the distinct impression that war clouds are gathering. The reason for the omnipresence of men in uniform is that, unlike most of their European contemporaries, Swiss men are obliged to complete military service. Under the militia system, some 155,000 recently-trained men are in theory ready to turn up for duty, armed and in uniform, at a moment's notice. In practice, mobilisation would probably take several days. Swiss recruits have the option of completing their military service all in one go over a minimum of 10 months (longer for higher ranks) or – what most choose to do – complete the initial 18 or 21 weeks of training, followed by annual stints of refresher training until the full service of (minimum) 260 days has been completed.

A sensible guarantee of neutrality is to make yourself an unattractive prospect for invasion. The Swiss have taken this to heart. In its first century of existence, war came close to modern Switzerland three times, beginning with the Franco-Prussian War in 1870. On each occasion the Swiss declared their neutrality and occupied their borders in force, successfully deterring the conflict. The Cold War also cast its long shadow on Switzerland, keeping the fear of conflict alive.

Far from being an oasis of peace and pacifism, Switzerland is one of the most militarised societies in Europe. There are no systematically-collected figures for gun ownership in Switzerland but it is estimated that the number of guns per 100 residents is 45, including weapons issued for military service (for which ammunition is not kept at home). This figure places Switzerland fourth worldwide, after the United States (112 guns per 100), Serbia and Yemen. Not Russia, not militarised Israel, but neutral Switzerland lands near the top of the gun-happy list.

With an army that costs five billion francs a year, the Swiss have created an advanced form of armed neutrality, which rests on strong military capability. You don't have to be a psychologist to see that the system is a hangover from the Second World War, when Switzerland was totally surrounded by Axis territory and feared imminent invasion, at least in the early years of the war. Like Scarlett O'Hara in the iconic scene from *Gone With the Wind*, who raises a clenched fist to the sky and swears, "I'll never be hungry again", the Swiss never want to feel unsafe again.

After the fall of the Iron Curtain, the Swiss bunkers and military manoeuvres started to look a bit over the top. But the Swiss never wavered. In September 2013, with the Arab Spring fresh in their minds and chaos in Greece threatening to destabilise the European Union, a total of 73% of voters rejected a popular initiative, put forward by pacifists and left-wing parties, to do away with compulsory military service.

Although the threat of land invasion is no longer the great fear, some Swiss defence tactics survived well past their use-by date. The military began mining bridges, tunnels and airfields at the start of the Second World War, and some of those explosives remained in place until well into the twenty-first century. The practice of setting demolition charges continued until the arms race of the 1980s and beyond. The process of demining Swiss transport infrastructure was only completed at the end of 2014. One of the last bridges to have explosives removed from under it was the thirteenth century wooden bridge in the small border village of Stein am Rhein, a popular tourist attraction, which attracts more than a million visitors a year.

While the legacy defence apparatus is slow to disappear, the Swiss are not exactly models of military preparedness. This was brought home in an embarrassing incident in February 2014 when the Swiss Air Force was unable to muster any planes in response to a hijacked Ethiopian Airlines aircraft headed for Geneva. The Swiss pilots hadn't turned up for work yet so it was left to the Italian and French air forces to escort the plane safely to Geneva. A Swiss Air Force spokesman explained that Swiss crews were only on duty during office hours, giving headline writers all over the world a field day. *Bloomberg* had the best fun: "Invading Switzerland? Try Before 8 or After 5".

Tainted trade

One fact that sits so uneasily with Swiss neutrality is the country's heavy involvement in the global arms trade. According to the Stockholm International Peace Institute, Switzerland is ranked fourteenth among the world's largest arms exporters in the period 2011 to 2015. In per capita earnings from the arms trade, the Swiss were ranked fifth in 2013, after Israel, Russia, Belarus, and neutral Sweden. In 2015, the State Secretariat for Economic Affairs approved war materiel exports valued at almost half a billion francs (CHF 446,550,281). On top of this amount, at least the same value of dual use or "special military goods", which includes military training aircraft and military simulators and arms and ammunition for civilian use, is sold

Swiss manufacturer RUAG, with 8,000 employees in nine countries and net sales of 1.7 billion francs in 2015, is a market leader in small calibre ammunition

by Swiss manufacturers each year. Germany is by far Switzerland's biggest customer, followed by a mixture of European and Middle Eastern countries. Saudi Arabia, subject to a ban on new export licences since the beginning of its bombing campaign in Yemen in March 2015, still purchased close to six million francs of the total that year.

Switzerland relies on end-user certificates to make sure that military equipment isn't re-exported by the receiving states but post-shipment verification is far from watertight. In 2012, Swiss-made hand grenades were discovered in Syria. They were part of shipment supplied to the United Arab Emirates in 2003, which were later transferred as a gift to Jordan without Swiss authorisation. This is not an isolated case. In recent years, Swiss arms have also resurfaced in Libya and Ukraine, and Swiss tanks, originally exported to Saudi Arabia, were used against demonstrators in Bahrain. On paper, Swiss weapons exports are banned to countries at war, or where there is a major risk that the arms are used to commit human rights violations. In practice, weapons can be purchased by belligerent countries before a conflict begins and replaced after a conflict ends, making this approach rather meaningless.

Over the past decade, weapons exports have made up less than 0.5% of total Swiss exports (in line with the value of arms traded annually as a proportion of total global trade), yet the industry is holding on to its niche, with the backing of the Swiss electorate. In November 2009, on the same day the Swiss voted to ban minarets, they also voted by a two-thirds majority against a proposal to ban arms exports.

On the other hand, Swiss neutrality is not mute; it does not preclude the Swiss from denouncing violence. The Swiss government condemns state and terrorist violence on a regular basis, including Islamic State atrocities or any attacks against civilians. It often condemns excessive force by Israel against the Palestinians, and more generally "the escalation of violence" between Israel and the Palestinians.

During the devastating 34-day Lebanon War in 2006, the Federal Department of Foreign Affairs issued a statement condemning "the disproportionate reaction of the Israeli Defence Forces in Lebanon". In 2011, Switzerland condemned the planned construction of several thousand additional housing units in East Jerusalem and neighbouring settlements, stating that "the colonization of the occupied Palestinian territory, both in East Jerusalem and the West Bank, is illegal and constitutes a violation of international law".

Switzerland has condemned nuclear weapons tests in North Korea; the 2015 coup in Burkina Faso; violence against Syrian citizens by state forces and the use of chemical weapons in Syria; executions in Iran; as well as Russia's annexation of Crimea, and its involvement in the conflict in eastern Ukraine.

Threats and dangers

Every few years the Swiss government releases a security report which looks at the global security environment and sets out Swiss strategies to deal with threats and dangers. Much changed between the last two reports of 2010 and 2016, with implications for Switzerland. The latest report identifies strained relations between Eastern and Western Europe, the terrorist threat of jihadism and risks of cyber-attack as the leading areas of concern.

The most unexpected change has been the worsening in relations between Russia and the West since events in Ukraine. The Swiss, who held the presidency of the Organisation for Security and Cooperation in Europe (OSCE) in 2014 when the Russians annexed Crimea and intervened militarily in Ukraine, clearly identify Russia as the aggressor.

Good offices

Name almost any major conflict around the world, from Sudan to Syria, and the Swiss will have a connection to it. An odd state of affairs for a neutral country? Not in the Swiss case, where neutrality has become an access-all-areas badge in the most embittered and protracted international clashes. The Swiss are neutral, in the sense that they go to great lengths to stay out of wars, but when it comes to international conflicts they are anything but passive. Swiss neutrality is not about sitting on the fence and staying silent. On the international stage, Switzerland regularly denounces aggression, imposes sanctions, and gets involved in peace-broking or good offices wherever there is a need.

In international relations, the term good offices refers to all third-party diplomatic and humanitarian initiatives seeking to resolve or overcome a bilateral or international conflict. Activities include mediation and facilitation, and taking on the role of protecting power mandate, or middleman.

Switzerland gained a wealth of protecting power experience during the Second World War when it represented the interests of 35 states – including the major warring powers – with over 200 individual mandates. The ultimate networking coup, it hasn't harmed Switzerland's economic and strategic interests to be so firmly enmeshed in everyone else's business. Good offices are part of Switzerland's strategy for survival, and have been profitable over the long term. Since Swiss neutrality was guaranteed by the European powers in the Treaty of Vienna in 1815, the Swiss have had reason to fear the spill-over of war on more than one occasion. For this important reason the country has traditionally sought to maximise its usefulness on the diplomatic front.

When states are at war or when they break off diplomatic ties, it leaves a vacuum where basic housekeeping needs such as consular services are disrupted. But however strong the mutual enmity is, a minimum of communication is essential to resolve certain problems. This is where Switzerland comes in, like the child of warring parents who passes requests and information back and forth. Switzerland's longest-running protecting power mandate was between Cuba and the United States, from 1961 to 2015. In this case, messages were sometimes a matter of avoiding World War III.

Like one in the middle of the Cuban missile crisis in October 1962: the Americans planned to send reconnaissance planes to verify that the Soviet missiles were, as the Cubans claimed, really gone, and they needed to use flares to see the locations. Fearing the flares could easily be mistaken for bombs, the US Secretary of State contacted the Swiss ambassador in Washington with the "don't shoot" message. The Swiss ambassador relayed the message to his counterpart in Havana, Emil A. Stadelhofer, who swiftly delivered it to Fidel Castro, with whom he enjoyed a good working relationship.

After the missile crisis ended, in 1965, Cuban dissidents were given the green light by Castro to leave the island under their own steam, resulting in a spate of drowning tragedies involving Cubans who were trying to reach the Florida coast in unsafe boats. Moved by the plight of the refugees, Stadelhofer

This photo of the Swiss registration of Cuban refugees was taken by Swiss photographer Luc Chessex, who lived in Cuba from 1961 to 1975, and worked for several years for the Cuban Ministry of Culture as an official photographer of the Revolution

pressed both sides for a better solution. Washington authorised him to negotiate an air route between Cuba and Miami for Cubans wishing to flee. John Hudson reported in *Foreign Policy*:

> By December, the Swiss had helped secure an agreement between Havana and Washington to provide two flights each day for five days a week enabling the departure of 3,000 to 4,000 Cubans monthly from the Varadero military airport. The arrangement held for the next seven years and became the most labour-intensive aspect of Switzerland's protecting-power mandate in Cuba.

By the time the Freedom Flights, to use the US description, came to an end, more than 260,000 Cubans had been airlifted to the United States, every one of them registered by the Swiss before they left Cuba. The Swiss kept their role as middleman for 54 years until the United States and Cuba finally celebrated the restoration of full diplomatic relations in July 2015. Switzerland's ambassador in Washington, Martin Dahinden, marked the occasion quietly at the Swiss embassy: in the presence of a handful of staff, he unscrewed a small gold plaque that identified the Swiss government as the protecting power of Cuban interests in the United States. A discreet end to a discreet role, in which Switzerland made a huge contribution to global stability and helped more than a quarter of a million Cuban refugees.

New opportunities

When one door closes, another one opens pretty quickly, or should that be the other way round? Soon after the gold plaques were removed from the Swiss embassies in Washington and Havana, new ones were required in Tehran and Riyadh. In February 2016 Switzerland agreed to represent Iran's interests in Saudi Arabia and Saudi Arabia's interests in Iran. Saudi Arabia broke off relations with Iran at the beginning of January 2016 after tensions following the execution of a Shia cleric in Saudi Arabia, culminating in the storming of the Saudi embassy by demonstrators in Tehran. Given the level of tension and animosity between these two key nations in the Middle East, this latest two-way protecting power role may prove Switzerland's most challenging to date.

Switzerland has several other mandates, notably representing US interests in Iran since 1980. One of the things that makes consular services for some 8,000 US citizens in Iran more demanding is the Iranian penchant for detaining them on spurious grounds. When three American tourists – two men and a woman – were arrested and imprisoned by Iran in

2009 after accidentally straying into Iranian territory while hiking in Iraqi Kurdistan, the Swiss ambassador Livia Leu Agosti and her staff visited them in captivity and tried to protect their interests throughout the legal proceedings against them. The Americans viewed their imprisoned citizens as hostages, while the Iranians convicted the hikers of spying. The day the final two Americans were released in September 2011, they were swept out of the prison in cars belonging to the Swiss and Omani representatives in Tehran.

In addition, the Swiss have hosted endless rounds of talks on Iran's disputed nuclear programme, finally leading to a breakthrough in July 2015 when six world powers reached a deal with Iran on limiting Iranian nuclear activity in return for the lifting of international economic sanctions. The full extent of the Swiss role in the rapprochement between the two countries may not emerge for many years.

With the lifting of sanctions, talk has now turned to economic opportunities in Iran, not just for Switzerland but for other countries too. No other Western country will be as well placed and well connected as the Swiss, who have sent several trade delegations to Iran over the years. A presidential visit by economics minister Johann Schneider-Ammann came in February 2016.

As Daniel Trachsler observed in his 2012 paper for the Center for Security Studies of ETH Zurich on protecting power mandates, the most important argument from the Swiss perspective in accepting a mandate is not necessarily peace support.

> On occasion, accepting mandates as protecting power also gives Switzerland itself good opportunities to pursue its own interests and to promote issues of its own …. As a protecting power, Switzerland enjoys access to the highest corridors of power. In a way, such mandates therefore open doors for bilateral Swiss concerns as well. Such advantages

also explain, for instance, why Sweden competed with Switzerland for the representation of Georgia's interests in Moscow and was far from pleased when Switzerland ultimately received the mandate.

An affair to remember

Easily the most extraordinary and difficult challenge faced by Swiss neutrality was the Libyan crisis, which lasted from July 2008 to June 2010. Up to that point Switzerland and Libya had enjoyed a mutually beneficial relationship. Members of the eccentric dictator's family liked to holiday and spend some of their limitless wealth in Switzerland, while the Swiss imported Libyan oil, and Swiss companies signed contracts for construction and infrastructure projects in the North African country. All that changed when the Swiss got on the wrong side of the Gaddafi family. At the peak of the crisis, Gaddafi called for a holy war against Switzerland and said the country should be dissolved. Meanwhile the Swiss were considering launching a covert raid in Tripoli to free hostages.

It all began with a visit of one of Gaddafi's sons to Geneva. Hannibal al-Gaddafi was staying with his family in a suite at the luxury Hotel President Wilson when he allegedly physically assaulted two of his domestic staff. Police arrested Hannibal and his pregnant wife. Both were detained for two days before being released on bail and allowed to leave the country.

Hearing of the incident, Muammar Gaddafi flew into a rage, shutting down the offices of Swiss companies in Libya and threatening to cut oil supplies to Switzerland. Within days, two Swiss businessmen based in Libya had been arrested on trumped-up visa charges – Max Göldi who worked for the Swiss engineering firm ABB, and Rachid Hamdani, who worked for a Swiss construction firm. The men became hostages for the next two years, spending most of that time in the sanctuary of the Swiss embassy and periods in Libyan custody. Göldi and Hamdani became household names in Switzerland as high-ranking political delegations made fruitless attempts to secure the men's release. A year in, the crisis was worse than ever and the Libyans withdrew billions from Swiss banks.

It is hard to say what the worst moment of the crisis was. In February 2010, Hamdani was finally given clearance to leave Tripoli, but Libya threatened to raid the Swiss embassy in order to arrest Max Göldi. Ambassadors from several EU countries gathered at the embassy in Switzerland's hour of need in a show of solidarity. Finally, Göldi agreed to give himself up and was taken to prison, while Hamdani was permitted to leave the country.

In the end an agreement was brokered by several countries, and a second Swiss presidential visit in June 2010 (Hans-Rudolf Merz had visited in 2009), this time by Micheline Calmy-Rey, ended in a deal that allowed the second hostage to return home. Spain's foreign minister and Italy's prime minister accompanied Calmy-Rey on her last visit. For the first time, Switzerland was forced to rely publicly on the good offices of others.

Diplomatic channels won out in the end, but the fact that the Swiss army prepared several plans for freeing the hostages from foreign territory – either across the desert or by sea – shows how close Switzerland came to bending its neutrality. Not all the cabinet ministers were aware of these plans, a fact which drew strong criticism when revealed, as it went contrary to the national principle of consensus decision-making.

The pipes of peace

As for legal military activities, Switzerland plays a modest role in international peace-keeping. It has a small number of military personnel on peace-keeping service abroad, most of them part of the 220-strong Swiss company (Swisscoy) stationed in Kosovo, deployed with NATO's Kosovo Force (KFOR) since

Change of command of the Swisscoy contingent at the airport in Pristina, Kosovo

1999. A further 20 soldiers are attached to the so-called Liaison and Observations Teams in Bosnia-Herzegovina as part of a European Union force. It has been the government's stated intention for several years to increase the number of Swiss troops involved in international peace-keeping duties to 500, but there is no sign of a move on that goal yet.

On the conflict resolution front, Switzerland has accompanied more than 20 countries in over 30 peace negotiations in recent years. It led its own mediation proceedings between Armenia and Turkey, and between Georgia and Russia, among others. In the past seven years, the Swiss Federal Department of Foreign Affairs has taken part in more than 15 peace negotiations, including Sudan, Colombia, Nepal, Myanmar, Sri Lanka, Mali and Syria.

The Swiss have had a special involvement in North Korea since the end of the Korean War in 1953, when Switzerland was appointed to the Neutral Nations Supervisory Commission, whose troops are stationed on the demarcation line between North and South Korea. This mission marked the first deployment of members of the Swiss Armed Forces abroad. Since then Switzerland has been active in peace promotion and humanitarian assistance efforts, and has hosted mediation talks between China, the United States and North Korea on numerous occasions. And don't forget, North Korea's new supreme leader, Kim Jong-un, was sent to school in Bern.

Closer ties

The Swiss worked hard for their neutrality and have put great effort into retaining it – making it a cornerstone of national identity. But the pledge to stay neutral towards all belligerents in future wars has had its drawbacks, as seen during the Second World War when the Swiss got caught in a position that led them to make heavy moral compromises (see Chapter 7).

In the era of globalisation, the Swiss are under no illusion that they can guarantee national security alone. Geography and distance may have helped in the past, but in today's world any country can be affected by events or developments that originate far from their own borders. The Swiss government's stated goal for the next five to 10 years is to promote closer and more intensive Swiss cooperation with international security organisations. Switzerland is a member of NATO's Partnership for Peace and has agreed to work more closely with Germany and Austria on political security questions related to the OSCE. The EU continues to be an important security partner. Bigger plans are also in motion. The Swiss government agreed in 2010 to apply for a temporary seat on the UN Security Council in 2023/2024. The decision will be taken by the UN General Assembly in 2022.

The Swiss have come a long way since they voted to join the United Nations in 2002, the first country to seek membership with the backing of a popular vote. Welcoming the yes vote, the Swiss government said it sent a "clear signal that Switzerland wants to commit itself to working with all other countries in solving world problems, be these poverty, suffering, illness or war". Whatever else happens, the Swiss pledge to help resolve conflict rather than joining it is here to stay.

In focus: Pascal Couchepin. "We are not the moral guardians of the world."
Retired former President Pascal Couchepin is a man without regrets. He made it to the top of the heap in his chosen field so why should he regret anything? he asks me. In a wide-ranging discussion held in a humble railway café, one of the most recognisable figures in Swiss politics of the past three decades gave me an insight into the world view of the Swiss establishment. Here is a selection of his comments on different topics.

The question of taking a moral stance against odious regimes: "We try to follow the moves of the international community. We are not the moral guardians of the world. Of course we shouldn't support immoral regimes – we are not going to sell ourselves – but we can't ignore the economic reality."

Swiss support for South Africa under apartheid: "Racial equality was not a general theme back then. Most of the population tolerated the Boers. They were Protestant and the Swiss Germans felt a link with them. At that time our main concern was to defend against Communism. That was the big fear. At that time defending against Communism was more important than the moral question."

The Swiss record in the Second World War: "We didn't save enough Jews – about 23,000 [saved]. We let the [German] trains through and we got food. We were not heroic. What would have been the point? We would have provoked Hitler and he could have eaten the Swiss for breakfast. We didn't pay the price in blood. We would have lost, according to General Guisan's report after the war."

The differences between Swiss French speakers and German speakers: "The Swiss Germans say *wir* [we] and have a strong sense of community. They like to be in a group singing together in the beer hall. That emotional fusion I don't like.

"The French-speaking Swiss are individuals at heart, we like to eat well and have a good discussion. We are 100% part of French culture. I don't mind being taken for a Frenchman."

Relations with the European Union: "Our attitude is that we are not doing badly without joining the EU. We have managed our affairs well. *Piano piano* [softly softly] with the EU is best. The Crusades took 150 years. Let it grow for another 100 years and see how they get on. Incidentally, if Switzerland joined the EU and the Union disappeared 100 years from now, I'm not sure we would remake Switzerland the same way."

The social injustices of the past: "I was the president of the local guardianship committee in Martigny [Couchepin went on to be mayor of his home town] at the age of 26. There was a very Catholic family who wanted their daughter sterilised because she had been pregnant. There were three of us in the committee and we said no.

"In another case there was a 22-year-old man who we interned because he was not willing to work. My cousin heard about this and said: 'Are you crazy?' So I had the man released and gave him to my cousin under guardianship [hearty laugh]. There was not much procedure involved – *tac, tac, tac* [Couchepin makes a chopping hand gesture to indicate efficiency]."

CHAPTER 7

The Swiss Helped the Nazis

"If soldiers [deserters] came in uniform, no problem. Anyone in civilian clothes was sent back. The Jews came and said: 'They're killing us'. But they all had to go back. The border guards were strict. They said they had orders. And there were tragic cases."

A young private in the Swiss army, Cla Famos, describes what he saw during the winter of 1943/1944 while home on leave in the village of Martina on the Austrian border. The border had been closed to refugees since September 1942 and the rule was being strictly enforced. Famos' family owned the Hotel de la Poste right beside the customs post, from where he witnessed many scenes between border guards and refugees.

More than half a century later, on film, Famos points to the bridge over the River Inn, where incomers from Austria were stopped and checked.

> Once, there on the bridge, we saw people on their knees begging to be allowed to enter. The poor sod [border guard], he wasn't permitted [to let them in]. Before they left, a woman tried to hand over her baby. "At least save my child," she said. The wife of one of the border guards and my mother were there, and this woman asked them to take the child.

The Swiss women did not take the child that day but Famos tried to help the refugees when he got the chance. "I would tell them to go back up and come around to the village from the other side." Famos was one of more than 500 people interviewed as part of the Archimob oral history project between 1998 and 2001.

The history of Switzerland and the Second World War has been picked over by commissions, committees and courts, by Swiss and international historians, by writers, filmmakers and journalists. Swiss neutrality in the face of Western Europe's most heinous crimes in history has inspired both praise and censure. If not for the Cold War, the Swiss would have come to terms with their failings much earlier. Instead, united against a new common enemy, the United Kingdom and the United States dropped their brief post-war interest in the rogue behaviour of the Swiss. At the same time the Swiss establishment was eager to gloss over its close economic ties with Nazi Germany, preferring to attribute the great Swiss escape to the country's courageous strategy of armed neutrality. In the intervening years, banking secrecy and selective memory helped draw a veil over the awkward questions.

It wasn't until the 1990s, after the collapse of the Soviet Union, that the questionable conduct of the Swiss during the war, and the poor record of the Swiss banks since the war, was revealed internationally, inspiring outrage.

The following exchange from a highly popular American satirical news show is a reminder of the judgments that have crystallised about Switzerland. On 3 December 2009 Jon Stewart's *The Daily Show* ran a segment on Switzerland, artfully mocking the vote to ban the construction of minarets, which had taken place a few days earlier. In his introduction, the host Jon Stewart referred to Switzerland as a "quaint gated community nestled in the heart of old Europe".

Then came the interview between John Oliver, award-winning English comedian and political commentator, and the
then Swiss ambassador to the United Nations, Peter Maurer,
on the theme of Switzerland's neutrality. Unwittingly, Maurer
had walked into a trap. Not only was he going to be used as
comic fodder, tricked into using the made-up word "dickish-
ness" at one point, he was going to be politically roasted over
Switzerland's role in the Second World War. The two-minute
edited version of the interview that was broadcast took a light-
hearted and even silly tone, until Oliver introduced the subject
of the war.

OLIVER: How hard was it to remain neutral during World
War II?

MAURER: Well, I think this is always a debate and I think we
do make a clear distinction between our neutrality
as an instrument of foreign policy and what we
think as individuals and what the country thinks.

OLIVER: But then, the neutrality issue seems complicated.
Now obviously, Hitler did some very bad things,
we know that. How do you focus on the positive
things to balance that out?

MAURER: It's not a question of positive. It's a question of our
neutrality has always been a state-driven concept
of not participating in war.

OLIVER: Was there not just a little voice of humanity inside
you saying this is terrible, we should really do
something about it?

MAURER: As a question of principle, it's unadvisable for a
country as small as ours to participate in war. Why
should we?

OLIVER: So: Easy to take a position on neutrality, hard to
take a position on Hitler.

MAURER: We did take strong positions on Hitler and many other things. We didn't participate in the war. That's two different things.

OLIVER: [imitating Hitler] "Would it be possible for me to keep my gold here?" [Imitating the Swiss] "Ah, Adolf! Of course! Lovely to see you again. Come back in! What have you been up to? Actually, don't tell me, I want to be able to say I don't know." [uncomfortable pause]

OLIVER: Is this neutral anger, or real anger, Mr Ambassador?

The Huffington Post ran an enthusiastic piece by Jason Linkins the next day, praising the journalistic courage of the interviewer. "Oliver used the news story to make a point about the overall character of the nation of Switzerland. Rather than take the glib remarks of Switzerland's UN Ambassador Peter Maurer at face value … he confronted the illogic and batted it back."

Sixty-five years after the war ended, some of the most influential new voices in US media can still link that behaviour to the "overall character of the nation of Switzerland". Is that fair? The perceived failings of leaders of other neutral or occupied European countries, including France, Spain, Sweden or Norway, or of the countries that fought alongside the Nazis, have not caught the public imagination in the English-speaking world in anything like the same way.

The Daily Show analysis drew from the World Jewish Congress-led campaign in the 1990s for Swiss banks to hand over assets of Holocaust victims. Swiss banks, which had squandered previous opportunities to respond fairly and adequately to the issue, agreed in 1998 to a $1.25-billion settlement of these claims. The media coverage around that time detailed instances of Swiss collusion with the Third Reich and lambasted the banks for their inhuman treatment of Holocaust survivors. Is there any worse charge in the Western world than having helped the Nazis? It is such a serious and damaging accusation that it demands a serious effort to separate fact from exaggeration.

There are two versions of the Swiss war story. In the first, the Swiss are villains who sold their souls for Nazi gold. The Swiss National Bank was the main recipient of gold from the Reichsbank, which included gold looted from the central banks of occupied countries. While the Swiss were accepting Nazi gold, they were turning away the victims of Nazi persecution, restricting the entry of Jewish refugees into the country. At least 20,000 desperate Jews were turned away between 1942 and 1944 when the borders were closed. Throughout this period Swiss factories were producing war materiel and other supplies for the Axis powers, delaying a potential Allied victory. There was no end to Swiss cooperation with the Nazis. The Germans were permitted to send goods trains, and possibly troops, across Swiss territory and through the St Gotthard rail tunnel to Italy.

The second story is a much more sympathetic one, one in which the Swiss, if not heroic, were at least plucky and resourceful. Faced with the threat of Nazi invasion, the Swiss kept their nerve. Rather than give up the hopeless fight before it even began, as other countries did, the Swiss carried out a mass mobilisation, calling up 450,000 men initially to defend the country's borders. The number of troops on active service fluctuated, dropping below 100,000 in the middle of the war. If it could not hold Hitler back at the border, the plan was to destroy transport lines, withdraw to fortifications in the Alps, and fight to the last man. By standing firm and maintaining its territorial integrity, Switzerland managed to provide shelter for hundreds of thousands of refugees and defeated soldiers, true to its humanitarian tradition. Every spare plot of land was

Volunteers of all ages report for duty in 1940

planted so that the Swiss could feed themselves. Switzerland remained the only beacon of independence and democracy in the continent's darkest hour.

And so which is it? Swiss profiteers, or an island of resistance in the heart of Nazi Europe?

Nazi Gold

During the Second World War the Swiss National Bank transferred 1.2 billion Swiss francs to the Reichsbank in exchange for gold, more than half of which had been seized by German forces from central bank reserves in occupied countries. A further 83 million francs' worth of gold was purchased by Swiss private banks, bringing the total trade to 1.3 billion francs. Of this total, almost 780 million represented looted gold from the Netherlands (400 million) and Belgium (378 million). On top of the gold trade, Switzerland also extended 1.1 billion francs in credit to the Third Reich to buy Swiss goods.

But what of Swiss dealings with the Allies? During the same period, the Swiss National Bank also supplied between 2.2 billion and 2.6 billion francs to the Allied governments in exchange for gold or dollars. Why did the warring nations want Swiss francs? Because, from 1941, it became the principal means of international payment. "The Swiss franc represented the best, and in some cases the only, means of payment for the belligerents on both sides to obtain certain products or services in countries outside the territories they controlled," Philippe Marguerat wrote in his contribution to *Switzerland and the Second World War*, edited by Georg Kreis (published in 2000).

In dispatches to Dublin, written on 10 April 1940, Irish diplomat Francis T. Cremins described the atmosphere in Switzerland. "There is general anxiety at the callous treatment to which neutral countries have been subjected, and the feeling is growing that the turn of Switzerland will come eventually. The Swiss continue, however, to feel fairly safe so long as Italy maintains her non-belligerency." Italy joined the war on Hitler's side two months later.

Between May and June 1941, France, Yugoslavia, Greece and the Baltic nations fell to the Nazis. Switzerland found itself a solitary free country completely surrounded by the Germans, their allies, or territory under German control, extending for hundreds of miles in all directions.

The Swiss army was no match for the Nazi war machine, as the drafted men quickly realised. Hans Wyman from Neuchâtel recalled that there were only one or two infantry cannons for the 800 men in his battalion. "The time I was really scared was when I saw the rest of our equipment. We'd seen their [the Germans'] magazine *Signal* and we knew what kind of tank units they had. Jesus, what could we have done?" That an open fight at the border would have been lost was tacitly acknowledged by the Redoubt plan, which involved pulling back to the mountains and leaving the civilian population to occupation. Nevertheless, the mobilisation was far from meaningless. Even if defence was only an illusion, it was a necessary illusion to quell the fears of the people and allow some form of normal life to continue.

For geographical reasons, Germany was traditionally Switzerland's largest trading partner. But why maintain and even increase trade with a regime that so brazenly breached Swiss democratic values? Behind almost all of Switzerland's decisions, some argue, was the overriding imperative to avoid the catastrophe of invasion. According to Marguerat, Switzerland kept up intense financial ties with Germany, including the purchase of gold known to be of dubious origin, for a range of reasons, beyond the threat of invasion. Economic war would pose a huge risk to Swiss survival as Switzerland had no raw materials of its own and relied on German deliveries of coal, oil and iron. Marguerat claims Switzerland needed the gold because it kept its currency secure. The strong franc was one of the main reasons Germany allowed a free Switzerland to exist. The Swiss could not afford to lose this usefulness. The second motivation for the trade in gold, and all other trade with Germany, it is argued, was that Switzerland was attempting to preserve its economic as well as political neutrality. Concessions to the Allies at the expense of the Germans would mean Switzerland was exposing itself to the wrath, and potentially the military might, of Germany.

Marguerat concludes:

> The SNB and the Swiss Confederation were in an inextricable situation. ... [They] tried to strike a 'balance of risks' to assure Switzerland's survival against the Axis and to gain the relative understanding of the Allies. This resulted in what could be described as a policy of financial neutrality, pro-

bably the only possible way out. And there was obviously nothing glorious or particularly moral about it at the time.

British historian Neville Wylie questions this reasoning. In his 2003 book *Britain, Switzerland and the Second World War*, he writes of the Swiss National Bank: "It is difficult to avoid the conclusion that its actions were motivated by neither questions of politics, nor a sense of service to the defence of the country, but rather by the desire to cash in on lucrative wartime business." Other Swiss historians, including Kreis, having drawn similar painful conclusions about the country's wartime record, find Marguerat's explanations to be too generous to the Swiss.

We know the Axis powers and the Allies secured large amounts of Swiss francs, but what did they spend the currency on? An estimated three-quarters of the money was spent on the war effort. For instance, the British purchased Swiss weapons and financed an extensive information network in Switzerland. British agents based in Switzerland could track the German economy and act as scouts for Bomber Command. The United States also had a notable presence in Switzerland through its Office for Strategic Services, whose role included organisational support for the French resistance and the identification of industrial targets in Germany. Switzerland was a hot bed of spies during the war. During those years 15 men, including three Swiss army officers, were executed by the Swiss for spying for the Germans, and more than 300 received prison sentences.

After the war, in May 1946, a Swiss delegation travelled to Washington to negotiate a resolution to the outstanding issue of Nazi gold so that economic relations could be normalised. After two months of tough negotiations, Switzerland agreed to pay 250 million Swiss francs of gold into the Western Allies' Tripartite Gold Fund for the reconstruction of Europe. This figure was a compromise, less than half what the US was seeking and more than double the initial Swiss offer. It was a no-fault agreement, in which Switzerland did not acknowledge any legal obligation in other respects. The agreement was a life-saver for Switzerland. The Allies also agreed to scrap the blacklisting of Swiss businesses, and the United States undertook to release Swiss assets in America, amounting to 4.5 billion francs, frozen since 1941. German assets in Switzerland were to be divided 50/50 between the Allies and the Swiss.

As part of the Washington Agreement of 1946, the Swiss made a secret commitment to identify assets in Switzerland belonging to heirless Nazi victims, in the course of compiling the inventory of German assets. "The resistance to this restitution measure, primarily emanating from the banks, was the prelude to the 'dormant accounts' scandal," Swiss historian Jakob Tanner notes.

Speculation that some of the gold received by Switzerland included gold stripped from concentration camp victims was not addressed in the Washington negotiations. It was not until the intense media focus on Nazi Gold and dormant accounts a half a century later that public allegations were made about the Swiss profiting from Holocaust victims' gold. In the light of the serious allegations, a 1997 US Department of State report was produced that looked into Switzerland's war record, and particularly the conduct of the Swiss banks and authorities regarding the unclaimed assets of Holocaust victims. The report was highly critical overall, but on the issue of victims' gold it was acknowledged that there was no basis to assert that the Swiss had knowledge of the provenance of such gold.

The issue of dormant or heirless accounts will be discussed later in the chapter. On the question of regular trade with the Nazis, this excerpt from a German government situation report about relations with Switzerland, dated 3 June 1943, shows how crucial the Swiss contribution was:

The Reich could not manage without the limited deliveries of supplies from Switzerland for a single month ... Swiss deliveries may only represent 0.5% of German supply capacity, but the products in question are particularly important technical special deliveries that significantly influence the tanks and remote control programme ... Economics Minister Funk explained that he could not manage for even two months without carrying out currency transactions in Switzerland ... The coal transports through the Alps should not be endangered, as they represent half the total delivery to Italy.

That this quote can be found in a textbook for 14-year-old pupils in Switzerland (Durch Geschichte zur Gegenwart 3) is a product of the openness inspired by the Bergier Report, a body of research produced by an independent commission of experts appointed by the Swiss government in 1996, amid a storm of bad publicity, to examine Switzerland's role in the Second World War. The commission, led by François Bergier, was given five years and 22 million francs to complete the challenge, and granted access to hitherto sealed archives. The report concluded that the Swiss authorities went beyond the limits of neutrality. More than that, the neutrality argument was often "improperly invoked to justify not only decisions made in all kinds of spheres, but also inaction on the part of the State".

Former IMF economist Helen B. Junz joined the commission towards the end of its mandate. In a 2003 essay, she noted that in the private sector, where transactions were not inhibited by considerations of neutrality, "a lot of business was done with an eye to profit only, without further thought to what adopting Nazi rules for doing business meant in ethical terms".

But did the Swiss contribution serve to prolong the war? Not according to the experts. "The Commission found no evidence of such an impact. Though access to Swiss resources could not be said to have been of no significance, it was also clear that, given the reserves remaining in the German economy and Germany's determination to continue to fight, the absence of Swiss cooperation could not have shortened the war in any material way."

Not only did Switzerland provide Germany with specialised products essential to the war effort, it also, as mentioned earlier, provided generous credit to Germany to finance its exports, to the amount of 1.1 billion francs. Transit cooperation also came into the mix. Switzerland allowed goods exchanged between Axis partners to transit through its territory. In return it could rely on essential German exports of oil, iron and coal. There was also a lively flow of secret exports to Britain. Research by British historian Neville Wylie has shown that the British Ministry of Economic Warfare procured more than 70 million francs' worth of undeclared materiel from Switzerland. Much of this was smuggled out by the British using elaborate scams, which often relied on Swiss officials turning a blind eye, as detailed in Sir John Lomax's 1965 book, *The Diplomatic Smuggler*.

Clearly, the economic ties between Switzerland and Germany ran deepest and were reflected in professional, financial and personal relationships that existed before the war and continue to this day. There were 150 subsidiaries of Swiss companies in Southern Germany alone during the war, employing an estimated 14,000 people, according to research by Sophie Pavillon.

"The model of maintaining an equidistant position between two camps in economic and financial policy could not hold up under conditions of war," Swiss historian Linus von Castelmur points out. Von Castelmur concludes that Switzerland fell inexorably into "Germany's gravitational field" between the summer of 1940 and the beginning of 1944.

Jewish refugees

The last living relative of Anne Frank was her Swiss cousin Buddy Elias from Basel. Buddy died in 2015 at the age of 89. Born in Frankfurt like his cousin, Buddy's story would have been very different had his family not moved to Switzerland in 1931 for his father's job. Anne's family took the fateful decision to move from Frankfurt to the Netherlands in 1933 and were safe for a while. Before the Nazi invasion of the Netherlands, the Franks made several visits to their relatives in Basel, and the young cousins, who were close in age, had great fun together.

"I'm sure that she would have become a marvellous writer. She would probably have also been very active in humanitarianism, working for the rights of women and children," Elias said in a 2009 interview with *swissinfo.ch*, to mark what would have been his younger cousin's eightieth birthday. Arrested in Amsterdam, Anne survived one winter in Bergen-Belsen concentration camp and died of typhoid fever in March 1945, a few months short of her sixteenth birthday.

Because Switzerland was not subject to the horrors of Nazi invasion, the small Jewish community in Switzerland, 20,000 in number, as well as Jews of other nationalities who found refuge in Switzerland during the war – an estimated 21,000 people – and those who were able to transit through Switzerland to safe countries, were spared the fate of persecution and deportation to death camps experienced by six million European Jews. That is something to be thankful for.

But it's not enough to look at what Switzerland did to help the Jews; we have to look at what it failed to do. Due to its longstanding neutrality, Switzerland had a tradition of taking in refugees, beginning with the French Huguenots in the sixteenth and seventeenth centuries. In the nineteenth century an asylum law was introduced to cater for the numerous political refugees – liberals, socialists and anarchists – who were turning up in Switzerland.

This humanitarian role was proudly promoted as part of Swiss national identity. Georg Kreis reminds us that the following announcement graced the central avenue of the 1939 Swiss national exhibition: "Switzerland as a refuge of the persecuted – that is our noble tradition. It not only expresses our thanks to the world for centuries of peace but acknowledges the great benefits brought to us over the course of time by homeless refugees."

So how was it that one year earlier, the Swiss had asked Germany to mark the passports of Austrian and German Jews with a red 'J'? The Swiss knew the Jews had compelling grounds to leave their Nazi controlled homelands, but they did not want to import a new Jewish population. Under Swiss asylum law, asylum was only offered to political refugees, excluding those persecuted on religious or racial grounds. Swiss police wanted to be able to identify and stop Jews who might be attempting to slip into the country. Indeed, wherever the German and Austrian Jews turned for refuge at that time, including the future Allied countries, they were met with closed doors or tight quotas.

Swiss President Kaspar Villiger issued a public apology for the treatment of Jewish refugees in 1995: "There is no doubt in my mind that our policy has brought guilt upon us. By introducing the so-called Jewish stamp, Germany was complying with a request made by Switzerland. At that time, in an excessively narrow interpretation of our country's interest, we made a wrong decision. The Federal Council deeply regrets this, and apologises for it, in the full knowledge that such a failure is ultimately inexcusable."

As mentioned, Switzerland was not alone in wanting to prevent an influx of Jews before and during the war. Britain maintained a quota system for refugees throughout the war, based

Over six days in June 1940, some 50,000 refugees crossed the Swiss border: 7,500 were French civilians, the rest were defeated French army soldiers (including 12,000 Polish nationals) fleeing capture. The French returned home after six months of internment but the Poles spent the rest of the war interned in Switzerland.

on the view that opening the doors to Jews would "stir up an unpleasant degree of anti-Semitism". The United States also enforced low quotas and did nothing specific to help Jewish victims of Nazi Germany until the War Refugee Board was set up in 1944. By this stage the Swiss had also relaxed their refugee policy, but it was too late to reach those most in danger.

In all, Britain accepted 90,000 Jewish refugees throughout the Nazi period, most of that number before the war under financial guarantee from the Anglo-Jewish community. The British government maintained that rescuing Continental Jews was not a war aim, even if such a thing were possible, and that the best way to save Europe's Jews was through Allied victory in the shortest possible time. Next door in neutral Ireland, the government made a deliberate and sustained effort not to take in any Jews throughout the period of Nazi persecution.

Member of the Federal Council from 1940 to 1951, Eduard von Steiger (1881–1962) was affiliated to the *Bauern-Gewerbe and Bürgerpartei* (Farmers' Traders' and Citizens' Party), forerunner of the Swiss People's Party

Switzerland accepted 295,000 refugees over the six years of the war. The total included 104,000 military internees (deserters, defeated soldiers, and crews of crashed military jets), 51,000 civilians (of whom 21,000 were Jewish), and 126,000 temporary visitors (including 60,000 war-zone children on three-month holidays). Refugees were obliged to hand over their assets to contribute to their upkeep, but they were not allowed to work in Switzerland. The different religious or political groups in Switzerland represented by the civilian refugees (socialists, Catholics, Jews) had to cover the rest of the costs.

The Second World War saw the greatest displacement of human beings in history. When the flow of refugees increased in 1942, when the Third Reich's "Final Solution" was fully implemented, the Swiss government decreed that conditions for asylum would have to be strictly enforced. In the words of cabinet minister Eduard von Steiger: "When you are in command of a small lifeboat with limited carrying capacity and supplies, that is already very full, while thousands of victims of a shipping disaster are crying for help, you must seem cold-hearted when you can't take everyone." Under this policy at least 20,000 Jews were turned away from Swiss borders.

Some Swiss citizens continued to help refugees with whom they came into direct contact and an unknown number of people were smuggled across the border throughout the war. Marguerite Constantin-Marclay from Valais was a young girl when she and her father came across a group of seven Jewish refugees hiding in the forest near their village, Champéry, on a Sunday in September 1942. The group had been left at the summit by a smuggler on the French side and warned not to fall into the hands of border guards. Constantin-Marclay and her father waited until dark to escort the two families down to their home in the village.

The Valais woman told her story to the Archimob researchers. "We didn't want anyone to see them. We were very secretive back then. We gave them something to eat and they had a wash and stayed the night. My mother spoke some German so we managed to communicate. There were two couples, one with two children and one with one child. They were from Amsterdam and had walked all the way. Imagine that."

The decision to adopt a hard-line policy was not unanimous. Parliamentarian and newspaperman Albert Oeri pleaded in parliament for a more generous approach to the crisis. "At the moment we can take really many more refugees without fear of hunger and unemployment … Our lifeboat is not yet overfull, not even full, and as long as it is not filled, let us take as many as we can."

In the end, the self-preservation argument won out and the government, which had emergency powers bypassing parliament for the duration of the war, adopted a cautious hard-line policy. As a direct result of this policy, the border guards in the village of Martina and at hundreds of other border posts were given a brutal role to play. What made this stance acceptable to the Swiss establishment and the population at large? The Swiss feared the presence of too many needy foreigners. They saw their jobs at risk – and their supplies of food as well. There was also the danger of provoking Nazi invasion. However, it cannot be denied that anti-Semitism contributed in some measure to Swiss cold-heartedness.

As for whether the Swiss populace knew about the mortal dangers Jews were facing, you have to ask: does it make a difference? The border guards who looked the desperate refugees in the eye must have known. Their superiors all the way up the political chain would have known. But as Kreis points out, and the current Syrian refugee crisis is a case in point: "The present day offers a wealth of examples to illustrate that one can 'know' a great deal and yet not perceive it as something that requires personal commitment."

The Geneva-based International Committee of the Red Cross (ICRC) tried to keep track of the deported and sought news of missing family members through the German Red Cross, then under Nazi control. It made inquiries in Berlin about the fate of hostages and deportees and it managed to send some relief items to camps and ghettos. Towards the end of the war some delegates were able to get into the camps to help rescue survivors. But by sticking to business as usual, the ICRC too failed the test of the times. When senior officials became aware of the genocide in the summer of 1942, the ICRC considered making an international appeal. It drafted a text criticising the conduct of hostilities, singling out the deportation, hostage-taking, and massacres of civilians, among other problems. The appeal text was considered by the committee in October, but ultimately they decided not to go ahead with it, believing such an action would be futile.

Speaking in 2002, a senior ICRC director François Bugnion admitted these efforts were a failure. "That they amounted to failure is undeniable, since the principles guiding the ICRC's work had never been so outrageously flouted. Millions of men, women and children died after a terrible ordeal without the ICRC being able to do anything to save them."

Dormant accounts

On 3 April 1936, the Reich Veterinarians Law expelled Jews from the profession. In October, Jewish teachers were barred from all public schools. Jews had already been barred from the legal and tax professions, editorial posts and the civil service. They had been stripped of their German citizenship. 1938 saw the Order for the Disclosure of Jewish Assets, requiring Jews to report all property in excess of 5,000 reichsmarks. The October 1938 Decree on the Confiscation of Jewish Property was followed a month later by a decree forcing the closure of all Jewish-owned businesses. In this dangerous environment, Switzerland, with its newly enacted banking secrecy law of 1934, was an obvious destination for worried Jews who wanted to preserve some of their assets.

Indeed Jewish families from countries all over Europe had accounts in Switzerland, especially those who ran their own businesses and travelled for work. Most of the account holders and their heirs disappeared during the war years, as the Jewish population of Europe was decimated by the Nazi genocide. But some managed to emigrate to safe countries in time and some survived in Europe against the odds. The cry – what happened to the money? – resonated for more than 50 years, until the Swiss banks agreed to settle US lawsuits for USD 1.25 billion in 1998.

"The history of Nazi victims' unclaimed assets in Switzerland is a history of neglected responsibilities," Swiss historian Peter Hug wrote in 2000, "accompanied by a recurrent and forceful media debate that comes and goes in cycles, invariably prompting the political authorities or the asset managers to take measures (which later prove inadequate)."

The problem with the Swiss approach before 1998 was that it was always based on self-assessment, relying on the goodwill and good faith of the banks. Between 1945 and 1962, the Swiss banking community made a number of efforts to identify assets on their books that had belonged to victims of Nazi persecution, each time reporting modest results. The 1962 survey, mandated by the Swiss government, came up with 6.2 million francs, seven times more than the survey that had been carried out six years earlier. Of this sum, 1.4 million francs was distributed to claimants and a further three million francs, from dormant accounts, was given to Jewish charities and refugee organisations.

Over the next decades the banks maintained, or some say hid behind, a policy of strict confidentiality. Claimants with inexact information were rebuffed, and the banks demanded death certificates for the owners of the accounts, making no allowances for the special circumstances, such as death in a concentration camp. In other cases they asked for money to process claims, or falsely claimed that records had been destroyed. Potential heirs or owners of accounts who lived behind the Iron Curtain had no opportunity to seek money that might be owed to them. Time dragged on.

If the banks assumed the problem would go away, they were wrong. The end of the Cold War and the fiftieth anniversary of the end of the Second World War brought renewed interest in the issue of Holocaust assets. Faced with a fresh wave of publicity alleging that the banks still held vast amounts of victims' assets, the banks announced a new, more exhaustive self-assessment survey.

This time round they identified 37.8 million francs' worth of assets belonging to foreign depositors who had not been heard from since 9 May 1945. But campaigners in the United States were not satisfied. In 1996 and 1997, a series of class action lawsuits were filed in New York against certain Swiss banks, alleging that the banks collaborated with and aided the Nazi regime by knowingly retaining and concealing assets of Holocaust victims. In the course of these lawsuits, the parties began settlement discussions.

One of the most hard-hitting examples of the extensive negative coverage of the Swiss around this time was an article that appeared in April 1997 in *The New Yorker*, entitled "Manna from Hell – Nazi gold, Holocaust accounts and what the Swiss must finally confront". Written by the magazine's European correspondent Jane Kramer, it was a scathing indictment of Swiss behaviour during and since the war. "The Swiss are wildly successful bankers, and the problems they are having now come at least in part from their behaving like bankers. They are rigid, they are greedy, and they are legalistically inhumane." So much for sweeping it all under the rug.

The parties reached an agreement in August 1998 to settle the lawsuits for USD 1.25 billion. Within the fund, a total of USD 800 million was destined for account holders and their heirs. The settlement also provided for survivors of Nazi German persecution, whether or not they had held accounts in Switzerland. In all, 457,000 Holocaust survivors and heirs received money from the fund, including 4,100 Jews who were turned away at Switzerland's borders during the war.

The World Jewish Congress could be satisfied that their work was done. "In exchange for the settlement amount paid by the Swiss banks, the plaintiffs and class members agreed to release and forever discharge the Swiss banks and the Swiss government from, among other things, any and all claims relating to the Holocaust, the Second World War, and its prelude and aftermath."

Where to now?

It is one thing to be released and forever discharged from any financial obligations, but will the Swiss ever be released from moral guilt? The journey of reflection was slow, but the Swiss have now acknowledged and apologised for their actions and inactions during that abominable time. Just as Switzerland's wartime Alpine bunkers are now open to the world, as museums, hotels, and even mushroom farms, its wartime record is open to be explored by anyone. Through the work of the Bergier commission, and decades of work by historians, the obligation of openness has been met. Swiss school children of the twenty-first century are no longer taught that the Second World War was their country's finest hour.

If Switzerland had its villains, profiting on the coat-tails of the Nazis, it had it heroes too – from ordinary citizens who helped smuggle and provide for refugees, to retired president Jean-Marie Musy, a former Nazi sympathiser who used his connections to try to rescue Jews from concentration camps. The Swiss person who made the biggest single contribution to saving lives was Carl Lutz, who used his position at the Swiss embassy in Budapest to procure safe passage for more than 50,000 Jews with forged documents. The Second World War was a cataclysm of death and suffering, one that the Swiss appeared to emerge from unscathed. As former President Pascal Couchepin puts it: "We didn't pay the price in blood." The good fortune of the Swiss has made it harder to forgive their flaws. But the Swiss did pay another price, a price of moral compromise that penetrated deep into the nation's soul, and it has taken generations to acknowledge and atone for those failings.

CHAPTER 8

The Swiss Are Boring

> Oh if you only knew, what a stupid, dull, insignificant, savage people they are! It is not enough to travel through as a tourist. No, try to live there for some time! But I cannot describe to you now even briefly my impressions: I have accumulated too many. Bourgeois life in this vile republic has reached the *ne plus ultra*.

Dostoyevsky again, complaining about the Swiss. Twenty-six Nobel prize winners later, Switzerland is the world's most competitive economy, second home of the United Nations, headquarters of the International Olympic Committee and the World Health Organization, global centre for commodities and finance, and location of the world's most expensive school, Le Rosey, at $120,000 per academic year. Times have certainly changed.

As for savage customs, some of the traditional celebrations enjoyed by the Swiss are a bit wild – whip-cracking, bashing strangers over the head with giant plastic hammers, effigy burning, and the wearing of grotesque masks to mention a few – but that outlandish behaviour is usually only seen one or two days per year. But one of the great Russian novelist's complaints remains: the infamous dullness of the Swiss.

In modern day Switzerland, things have become a lot more civilised, and politeness is highly valued. Greeting and parting rituals can't be ignored without causing offence. This code of behaviour is more formal than the norms in English-speaking countries, but is it tedious? Children as young as two are taught to shake hands with guests who come to their homes. It comes naturally to kindergarten children to say goodbye to their teacher by shaking hands. The whole country was offended by a case in Basel where two teenaged Muslim boys were excused on religious grounds by their school from shaking hands with female teachers. Even Justice Minister Simonetta Sommaruga weighed in on the controversy, claiming "shaking hands is part of our culture". Kissing, she might well have added, is also part of Swiss culture. Unless you can lose yourself in the crowd, there is no such thing as waving to the room when you arrive at a party. Women have the heavier kissing burden in Switzerland. At a social gathering they have to kiss everyone with whom they are on vaguely friendly terms on arrival and departure. Not just one kiss on the cheek, but three. At a party of 10 people, that's 60 kisses! The men at least can get away with shaking hands with other men. Apparently this kissing frenzy has evolved from more selective kissing customs in older generations. Who knows where it will end.

You will never begin a meal, no matter how humdrum the setting, without being wished *bon appetit* or *en guete*. Before taking the first sip of your drink you must clink glasses with everyone within reach, making eye contact with each person, never crossing hands with other clinkers. At the end of even the most casual of social exchanges, such as a postman handing you a parcel, it is customary to wish each other a good day, a good afternoon, a good evening, a good weekend, or a good whatever the upcoming festivity might require. Punctuality is not something the Swiss have to think about. To them it is just the norm; keeping people waiting for you is bad manners.

Most civilised of all, Sunday is a day of rest. The shops are closed and the lawn mowers and bottle banks are silent, by law.

As someone who lives very close to a bottle bank, I'm particularly grateful for that Sunday break. One morning a week when I won't be disturbed by early risers smashing bottles. No small matter in a country of recycling champions.

Do not disturb

Individual freedom trumps most things in Switzerland, after all this is the country where assisted suicide is calmly accepted as a matter of personal choice. But freedom stops where noise is concerned, which has a lot do with Swiss living conditions. The majority of the population is concentrated in the central plateau or lowlands, which is only a third of Swiss territory. Far from being surrounded by meadows, the Swiss live in one of Europe's most densely-populated areas, and most of them live in apartments. One in five is exposed to harmful and disturbing road traffic noise during the day. Because the working day starts early, often before eight o'clock, the freedom to sleep peacefully is jealously guarded.

If an excess of regulations is a sign of being boring, the evidence against the Swiss is strong. In a country where almost the entire adult male population has undergone military training, rules are accepted as part of life. Prescriptions on what noise is permitted or not permitted can be found in rental law, apartment block rules, in federal civil law, in local police regulations and in cantonal regulations. Generally, most areas have "quiet times" when restrictions on noise-making are more strictly enforced. Night quiet time varies but is usually in force between 10pm and 6am. Sundays and bank holidays are all-day quiet times, and, on working days, a midday pause in noise is to be respected between 12pm and 1pm.

The canton of Geneva provides an English translation of the local noise regulations to educate new residents on what is acceptable and to clear up some of the urban myths, such as the one about men being forbidden to urinate standing up after 10pm (number nine in "ten of the wackiest Swiss laws", courtesy of *timeout.com*). In fact there is a bathroom night ban, but it applies only to taking a bath or a long shower, because of the disturbance water might cause draining through the pipes. It is also forbidden during these hours to use a vacuum cleaner, move furniture around, play amplified music, or do noisy DIY jobs. Even people with their own plot of land are faced with noise restrictions. It is not permitted to use a powered lawn mower on Sundays or public holidays or on any day too early or too late (generally before 8am or after 8pm).

On Sundays there is no doubt that Swiss street life is eerily quiet. With some exceptions, such as at train stations or petrol stations and in certain holiday resorts, shops close on Sundays. In fine weather, café terraces and tourists bring life to city centres, but you could drive through several villages without spotting a single human being. Where are all the people? Most likely out pursuing the national past-time – walking. Switzerland is served by an integrated network of sign-posted hiking trails and pathways, maintained by the Swiss Hiking Trail Federation and protected by the Constitution.

Lukas Zbinden, the eponymous character in Christoph Simon's novel *Zbinden's Progress* is a frail elderly widower living in a retirement home who loves to talk and loves to go for walks. Lukas both embodies and subverts the Swiss stereotype. On the surface he has led such a conventional life – army recruit, schoolteacher, married father-of-one, enthusiastic walker – but at heart he's a revolutionary. At one point Zbinden muses on his favourite activity:

> Do you know what it means to go for a walk? Going for a walk is: acquiring the world. Celebrating the random. Preventing disaster by being away. Speaking to the bees

When you see this sign, you know you are on the right path

though you're already a bit too old for that. Not being especially rushed on a street that's like an oven in the afternoon sun. Missing the tram. ... Going at your own pace.

At your own pace you can criss-cross the country on 65,000 kilometres of pathways and backroads without ever having to worry about right-of-way. The hiking trails pass through forests, along country lanes, across fields, over rivers, through farmyards, all made easy by yellow lozenge-shaped signs to guide the way, painted on trees, stones and barns. The fact that these routes have been mapped out makes life easier for walkers and makes the countryside more accessible, which is a wonderful thing. But it also represents a taming of the environment. When every country lane is manicured, forest paths are cleared by workers wielding leaf blowers, and there are picnic tables, outdoor grills or chalets serving refreshments every few miles on mountain tracks, the experience of being in nature is somewhat stage-managed, and when you go to a popular spot – very crowded.

This desire to organise or regulate human activity reveals the wide cautious streak in Swiss society. Safety is often the overriding concern, at the expense of spontaneity. Until 2012 you couldn't just buy a bicycle in Switzerland and take it for a spin. First, you had to purchase annual cyclists' insurance and put the sticker on the bike. This would cover any damage you might cause in an accident. The only reason the bike insurance was scrapped was because the vast majority of Swiss citizens have civil responsibility insurance, to cover any damage to property they might inadvertently cause, and this was deemed to be adequate to cover bicycle liability. The Swiss are the most insured nation in the world, with the highest per-capita spending on life insurance and insurance premiums overall. The average Swiss resident spent USD 7,701 on insurance in 2013. That's around 50% more than in Japan, and around 75% larger than the spending on insurance per head in the US. Things that might be left to chance or people's own initiative in other countries are tightly controlled. Accident insurance is compulsory, as is health insurance. Some 2.5 million people have a form of air ambulance insurance through donations to the well-known provider Rega, whose red and white helicopters are a familiar sight on Swiss ski slopes. Every new house with a fireplace is listed and has to have an annual inspection and service by a certified chimney sweep (rules vary by canton), who is trained and registered and has the right paperwork.

If you want to keep a dog, be prepared to pay annual dog tax of at least a hundred francs. Needless to say, all dogs are registered, microchipped (since 2007) and have a health passport. Owners are fined if their dog strays and is picked up by the police. At least you don't need to carry plastic bags around with you to pick up after the dog, as the tax goes towards installing plastic bag dispensers wherever they might be needed. Under animal protection legislation, if you want to keep an animal classified as a social animal, such as a hamster or guinea pig, you will be obliged to keep at least two at a time so they have each other for company. But you might need to check your neighbourhood regulations first – ours forbids the keeping of rabbits or hens.

Three suns

The *Concise Oxford Dictionary* defines boring as "uninteresting, tedious, dull". Where does Swiss efficiency fit in here? The Swiss maximise every bit of their landscape to get the best possible use out of the available resources, a Nigerian student attending a course at the Swiss Institute of Federalism once remarked to me. Swiss neighbours returning from a holiday in Ireland were perplexed by the absence of orchards, vegetable gardens and forests on that island. They couldn't understand why the land wasn't being fully exploited.

On the journey from Lausanne to Montreux you will pass by Lavaux, a 30-kilometre stretch of terraced vineyards on the south-facing northern shores of Lake Geneva that dates back to the eleventh century. UNESCO explains its designation as a World Heritage Site like this:

> It is an outstanding example of a centuries-long interaction between people and their environment, developed to optimize local resources.... The Lavaux vineyard landscape demonstrates in a highly visible way its evolution and development over almost a millennium, through the well preserved landscape and buildings that demonstrate a continuation and evolution of longstanding cultural traditions, specific to its locality.

A few years ago I had the good fortune to go to the village of Cully in Lavaux to meet a family of wine producers – Les Frères Dubois. The three generations of Dubois men who collaborate in running the business were at the vineyard that day. Grandfather Marcel, the son of a vineyard labourer and a harvest grape picker, has the perfect wine pedigree. From humble beginnings – Marcel's first harvest in 1947 produced 1,000 bottles – the winery grew to be a thriving business, producing 1,000,000 bottles a year.

Over a glass of white, Marcel and his son Christian, both dressed in scruffy work clothes, reminisced about the old days and talked wine business. It was harvest time, and Christian's sons were busy out on the terraces. All hands are needed for the two weeks of the *vendanges*. The topography in Lavaux makes mechanisation impossible so the picking has to be done by hand.

Christian took me for a tour in a small jeep, zipping around the narrow roads between the terraces, where we saw the seasonal labourers and various members of the family at work, and I stopped to take some photographs of the stunning view over the lake. He explained the three suns of Lavaux – the sun overhead, the reflection of the sun's rays from the lake and the glare coming from the stone walls. We dropped in on the women who were preparing a slap-up midday meal. Everybody was so charming and industrious, it was like arriving in Swiss paradise.

This is just the sort of prosperity, efficiency and harmony that some observers find boring about Switzerland. In a 2015 piece entitled "Why 'happy' is boring", the *Financial Times* columnist John Kay expressed his chagrin at the Swiss being named the happiest nation on earth in the United Nations' World Happiness Report. Focusing on the quality of life in Swiss cities, he pointed at what he felt was missing – these places did not lift the spirit:

> Security, hygiene, good public transport – the factors that enter the assessment of liveability – are necessary for a fulfilling life, but they are not sufficient for it. That is why so

many young people from Melbourne or Toronto go to London or New York in search of the excitement and creativity of the great, rather than the liveable, city. [...] There is more to the good life than clean water and trains that arrive on time.

Make love not war

Lenin, former resident of Zurich, frowned upon the idea, embraced by some young communists, that sex should be as freely available as a glass of water. The Swiss seem to be more receptive to the suggestion, reporting the highest rate of satisfaction with their sex lives, ahead of Spain, Italy, Brazil and all the English-speaking countries, in the Durex Sexual Wellbeing Survey. The Swiss reported having sex on average 123 times per year, well above the global average of 103 times, and above countries like the United States (85 times) and the United Kingdom (92 times). How's that for boring? The 2008 survey interviewed 26,000 people, aged 16 and older, across 26 countries, and found that countries, like Switzerland, where people were more socially liberal about sex tended to have lower rates of sexually transmitted diseases, teen pregnancies and abortions. At eight pregnancies per 1,000 girls aged 15–19, the Swiss have the lowest teen pregnancy rate in the world. The rate in the United States is seven times higher at 57 per 1,000, while the rate in England and Wales is 47 per 1,000.

On the surface of things, the general lack of danger, deprivation and unpredictability in Switzerland could be used to make the case that the people are boring. To make matters worse, the strong national work ethic upsets the teenager in us. It will come as no surprise that the Swiss work longer hours than their European neighbours – a 42-hour working week, compared to an average of 35 hours in the EU. When given the choice in a 2012 referendum to increase statutory annual leave to six weeks for all workers, the Swiss said no, they were happy to stick with a minimum of four. In practice many workers get five weeks' annual vacation.

But are the people living in such a structured society inherently less interesting and less fun to be around? In group settings the Swiss may display a lack of exuberance. The exceptions to the rule are the traditional festivals, where people cast off their everyday reserve and go crazy, dressing up in wild costumes and carousing all night, especially around carnival time. *Chienbäse*, the torch-lit procession that takes place in Liestal, Baselland on the Sunday after Ash Wednesday, has become famous for its huge torches and bonfires. The procession starts with pipers and drummers marching with lantern bearers. They are followed by men and women carrying enormous burning wooden torches, each weighing up to 80 kilos. These events are a licence to have fun.

What about that peace and prosperity? This magic combination has brought continuity to Switzerland in a way that is difficult to match in other countries, especially Russia. Historically, most of the fighting done by Swiss mercenaries happened long ago and far from home in other people's wars, and with the exception of the difficult period at the end of the eighteenth and beginning of the nineteenth centuries, the Swiss peasantry did not have to suffer the ravages of invading armies or despots in modern times. The Swiss may have kept slaughter at bay and eschewed the expansionist and colonial aspirations of their neighbours, but has their caution turned them into the bores of Europe?

Or to use the words of Orson Wells in the role of Harry Lime in *The Third Man* (the hackneyed quote is compulsory for every English-speaking journalist writing about the Swiss), comparing Switzerland unfavourably with the Borgias of Florence: "In Switzerland they had brotherly love, they had five hundred years of peace and democracy and what did they produce? The cuckoo clock."

This put-down, which has shown great longevity in the English-speaking world, speaks volumes about the prevailing prejudice against Switzerland. The Swiss contribution to mankind has nothing to do with a Black Forest souvenir. More than any of its great scientists, architects, writers and artists, it is the humanitarian Henri Dunant, founder of the International Committee of the Red Cross and a contemporary of Dostoyevsky's, who stands out as Switzerland's all-time international high-achiever.

Dunant was in northern Italy on business when he witnessed the horror of the aftermath of the battle of Solferino in 1859. Shocked at the plight of the wounded and dying being left to cope on their own, he single-handedly organised a relief-effort there, wrote a book about his experiences and travelled Europe lobbying political leaders to change attitudes to the war wounded. Within a phenomenally short space of time, his campaign led to the signing of the First Geneva Convention by 12 states in 1864, the basis "on which rest the rules of international law for the protection of the victims of armed conflicts". For the first time in history, military leaders were forced to consider the welfare of wounded and captured soldiers, to treat them like human beings. Dunant became the first recipient of the inaugural Nobel Peace Prize in 1901.

Let's talk

Privacy has special importance in Switzerland, and not just for financial matters. With strangers, the Swiss are reluctant to pry and even more reluctant to reveal much about themselves, a constraint which hampers conversation. But this reticence does not apply to every situation and certainly not to close friendships. Everyone has a story to tell, if they can find the

Switzerland is famous for its clean streets, thanks to workers like Michel Simonet

right channel, and it won't be what you expect. Michel Simonet, a street sweeper in Fribourg, known for always going about his work with a rose on his cart, delighted the residents of the city when he wrote a book about his life, *Une rose et un balai* (A Rose and a Sweeping Brush). The father of seven who quotes Rabelais promised to follow Cézanne's example and "think with a brush". Part memoir, part philosophical musings, interspersed with poems, the book became a local bestseller, opening readers' eyes to the world of the "street technicians" who keep Switzerland so famously clean.

> A free head and busy hands suits me better, by the way, than the inverse. You think and exert yourself at the same time. Streets and squares are my gym, my solarium on fine days. I sing there like a cicada while working like

an ant, with open skies as my only limit, and a direct line to Our Father. [...] This harmonious balance between magnitude and intensity, action and contemplation, enthusiastic élan and habit, know-how and knowing how to be, of public relations and solitude is played out over a full day.

Simonet tells of the hardships of getting up for work at 4.40am and enduring the cold winter mornings outdoors, as well as being at the raw and dirty end of urban behaviour. But the book is much more an affectionate ode to his town and its people. He describes the frequent acts of kindness and solidarity that are part of his working life: the old widow Irène, always accompanied by her dog Gasparine, who invited Simonet and two colleagues to eat lunch in her grand apartment several times a year. The characters of Fribourg are immortalised in these pages, including a former colleague nicknamed Tulip, who took two beers fortified with shots of apple schnapps for his morning break at 9am – one for each leg, he used to say.

Frequenting the same cafés or restaurants is a very Swiss habit. *Stammtisch* is probably the setting where the most relaxed conversations take place between the Swiss, but I've only ever been privy to one of these meetings. A *Stammtisch* is a standing weekly arrangement for a group of friends to meet in a bar or café. The group always sits at the same table, and whoever can make it just turns up. It is particularly popular among retired people and a great way to keep up social contact. Some people attend more than one *Stammtisch*, meeting with different groups of friends.

While researching a story about the oversupply of hospitals in Switzerland, I found myself wandering around the quiet Swiss village of Saanen in the Bernese Oberland looking for local people to interview. The village hospital had been closed down two years earlier. I went into the bakery and asked the young Portuguese woman behind the counter where I could find some people to talk about the hospital. "Go to Doris's café," she said. "You'll find a *Stammtisch* there." Sure enough, I walked into Doris's *Kaffeestube* to find a jolly group of nine or 10 older men and women quaffing white wine at 11.30 in the morning. They squeezed around to make room for me and someone ordered an extra glass of whatever they were drinking. It turned out one of the women had worked at the hospital when she was young. They all had strong opinions about the closure, which they were happy to share with me. Stories of broken legs and births at the hospital followed, how great the doctors were, the way you could see your home from the upper floors when you looked out of the window. One man with excellent English told me about his travels in Afghanistan as a hippy in the 1960s.

A glass or two of wine before lunch? This is not unusual when the Swiss socialise. Loathe as I am to equate alcohol consumption with fun, it has been rumoured that there is a link between the two. The Swiss consume more alcohol per capita than the EU average, the equivalent of 100 bottles of wine or 200 litres of standard beer per year. This could be taken as a sign that the Swiss are partying, although who can say whether or not their partying is boring. It is not against the law to drink in public spaces, and you will see people in parks or by the lake drinking. However, there is certainly nothing like the messy public drunkenness I am used to seeing in Britain or Ireland. The Swiss have a more relaxed attitude to alcohol consumption. From the age of 16, young people can be served beer or wine in a bar. The minimum age rises to 18 for spirits. With two-thirds of school leavers choosing the apprenticeship path to employment, where they combine days of on-the-job training with days spent in class in a vocational college, this means not only may you be served by a 16-year-old apprentice in the bank, you may meet the same adolescent out later having a perfectly legal (but possibly boring) after-work drink.

The eternal flame

Stability and continuity could be construed as boring, but they do bring fascinating depth and richness to a culture. Where else but in Switzerland would a fourteenth century murder lead to a twenty-first century court case?

The *Jahreszeitbuch* was a record kept by Catholic parishes of the names and dates of death of parishioners or other important dates to be commemorated. This is an extract from the *Jahreszeitbuch* of the small village of Mollis in canton Glarus, eastern Switzerland, dated 9 July 1357:

> So, Konrad Müller from Niederurnen has pledged, for the uncaring killing of Heini Stucki, to burn an eternal lamp day and night using nut oil from his property, namely [detailed list] ... and if the aforementioned light is not lit all of the above goods belonging to Konrad Müller will be forfeited to the Church.

Was it influence or eloquence that got Müller off the hook for his terrible deed? We will never know. Nor were the details of the murder recorded, but the pledge made in 1357 remained with his descendants and their land for the next six centuries. Think about that for a second: a community so law-abiding and orderly, so untouched by upheaval, that a bond of this kind could be honoured for so long. For 600 years, successive generations of owners of what was once Konrad Müller's land paid the cost of lighting the lamp. At first it was nut oil; in later years, candles were used.

No one rebelled, no one forgot. Not even the Reformation interrupted the arrangement. When Mollis became Protestant 200 years after the murder, the lamp was simply moved to St Hilarius, a catholic church in the nearby town of Näfels and it was business as usual until one day in 2009 when a new owner inherited the land.

Around this time the church wanted to enter the payment bond into the land register in the amount of 70 francs per year. When the farmer refused to comply, the church assembly voted to pursue the matter in court. The farmer came up against a certain amount of hostility in his community, according to his lawyer, but the local cantonal court found in his favour, awarding costs to the farmer and cancelling the arrangement forever.

The eternal lamp in Mollis is an extreme example of Swiss conservatism and the old traditions that have survived under the peculiar conditions that exist in Switzerland. Many other timeless customs are still observed, activities that feel like they come straight from the Middle Ages because they genuinely do go back that far.

Tough decisions

Switzerland is a safe country, the kind of place where street harassment of women is the exception rather than the rule, and the president can blend in with other commuters on a train station platform and not be bothered by anyone. But the Swiss are not all about staying within safe boundaries. Thanks to the system of direct democracy, voters express themselves regularly at the ballot box, and when it comes to social problems, they have shown themselves willing to try radical solutions.

The scourge of heroin grew so bad in the 1980s that 1% of the young adult population was addicted to the drug. There was a public outcry at the scale of open drug-taking in the cities, especially the infamous "Needle Park" in Zurich, not to mention the unnecessary deaths and crime. The pragmatic Swiss solution, accepted by popular vote, was to go on a therapy offensive, introducing a massive methadone distribution programme nationwide along with prescribing medically controlled heroin to a small minority of severe addicts, an approach that worked but is still too radical for most countries. Drug-related crime disappeared almost overnight.

Swiss law also permits assisted suicide under pretty loose conditions, the main proviso being that whoever assists the person seeking to die cannot benefit in any way from the death. The right to die has consistently been backed by the electorate and the two main assisted suicide organisations help some 1,000 people annually to end their own lives by drinking a lethal dose of barbiturates.

The most difficult conversation I ever had in the course of my work was with a woman in her 50s whose mother had died through assisted suicide. Let's call her Sabine. I arrived at Sabine's home in a large 1980s apartment complex on the outskirts of Bern, in one of those charmless suburbs of low-rise housing you often come across in Switzerland. Not a cheap area by any means, just a little faded. Inside, the apartment was spacious and immaculate, with a mezzanine layout and lots of light. My barefooted hostess was dressed in a black fitted dress.

Sabine made some herbal tea, and we sat down at the dining table to talk about a very difficult time in her life. I asked her to describe her mother's state of health before she died.

> My mother was frail but not in pain or terminally ill. Nevertheless, she was suffering. She'd had a stroke three years earlier and had mobility problems and difficulty speaking. That was the hardest thing for her, not to be able to express herself, because she was a poet and loved language.

The old woman had resisted going into a nursing home, or any offers of home help. "I organised carers to visit but she turned them away." But after two falls at home, she agreed she needed proper care and went to live in a nursing home. Unfortunately, she was not happy in the new living arrangement and began to talk about ending her life.

"It took me several months to accept that my mother's wish was genuine and that I would have to facilitate this wish. I would say to her, you're depressed, give it time, but she would become upset with me for denying her feelings, as she saw it."

In the end, Sabine relented. She contacted the relevant organisation on her mother's behalf to begin the whole process of assessment and planning. On the day of her death, Sabine's mother wanted to go for a family lunch, including her ex-husband in the group. Sabine was too upset to accompany her parents and brother to the restaurant, and she stayed at home to wait for the end.

> I didn't want my mother to die in an anonymous apartment in Zurich [provided by the assisted suicide organisation] and the nursing home management would not allow the suicide to take place there. So I agreed to have her die here. My mother was so relieved that she could be somewhere comfortable and familiar. They came back from lunch shortly before the representative of the assisted suicide organisation arrived. She did not want any fuss; no flowers, no music. She just wanted to get it over with.

There is great respect for self-determination and individual responsibility in Switzerland, which allows people to make interesting choices and potentially live more fulfilled and less boring lives. At the funeral Sabine and her brother were open about how their mother had died and received a supportive response from those attending.

This respect for individual choice makes the Swiss reluctant to limit the freedoms of their fellow citizens. However, other less compassionate decisions have been made regarding the freedoms of foreigners in their society, especially when it comes to any perceived threat to the peace and security so dearly cherished by the Swiss.

In superficial interactions with the Swiss, newcomers will be struck by their controlled politeness, reserve (apart from all the kissing) and fixed ideas about how things should be done (make no mistake, the silent compartment on the train really is meant to be silent). These traits, much less evident in the younger generation, speak of a need for a safe framework in which to live. But it is a mistake to allow your knowledge of the Swiss character to stop there. The reserve is not permanent, the polite greeting and parting does not exclude having fun in between, and they would never have progressed to this point, socially and economically, without being open to new ideas. The Swiss will never be the wild child of Europe; you only have to look at their lovingly tended vegetable patches to see that. But whether they are boring or not most likely depends on the eye of the beholder.

In focus: Rainbow family

Maria von Känel and her partner Martina have been a couple for 18 years, and are raising their two children, a boy and a girl, together. When civil partnership for homosexual couples was introduced in 2007, the couple were among the first to register their partnership. But they had to wait until 2016 for parliament to grant the right to adopt each other's children and gain parental rights in case of separation or the death of one partner. At the time of publication, they were still waiting for the law to come into force, and hoping it would not be challenged by referendum. Until now, gay people in a co-parenting relationship have been barred from adopting their partners' children (step-child adoption), even though regular adoption was open to homosexuals who applied as a single person. This anomaly has caused great anxiety among so-called rainbow families – families with at least one parent who is gay, lesbian or transsexual. Von Känel, who is co-founder of the Swiss Rainbow Families Association and NELFA (Network of European LGBTIQ* Families Associations), says there are between 6,000 and 30,000 children growing up in rainbow families in Switzerland.

How are things different for them? "The difference between us and heterosexual parents is that we have to make an extra effort in relation to awareness. The coming out process is ongoing and demands energy. Although we are still not legally recognised as a family according to Swiss law, social acceptance is high in Switzerland. In comparison, things are lagging behind at the political level." While gay marriage has now been introduced in 12 Western European countries, things are moving more slowly in Switzerland, although seemingly in the same direction. The issue of marriage equality is currently before parliament in the form of an initiative ("Marriage for all") submitted by Kathrin Bertschy of the Green Liberal Party, but voters will have the final say.

Von Känel finds that people are very curious when they come into contact with her family for the first time. "I often experience that they really have the need to share with us that they find it good and stand behind us. And that has always given us a lot of strength." The couple, who live in a village near the city of Zurich, have always been open about their family model with carers, teachers and fellow parents in day care, kindergarten and school. "The teachers took that on board very well. They used books that presented different types of families to introduce the subject to the children, and that gave our children confidence. It was not only our children who benefitted but also children from one-parent families and step-families, or children being brought up by their grandparents."

"The times that are a challenge for us as a family are when voyeuristic reports about gay parents appear in the media. Then we are confronted with prejudice. But through our association we have been able to combat very many prejudices over the past years."

Von Känel hopes not to have to wait too long for marriage equality, as marriage is a long-held wish for her relationship. "We don't want any special rights, we just want the simple rights, the same rights. We have been encouraged by the failure of the 2016 tax initiative brought by the Christian Democrats. It was actually an initiative about fair tax treatment for married couples compared to co-habiting couples. The initiative was rejected and one of the reasons it failed was that it included a definition of marriage as a union between a man and a woman. Had this wording been enshrined in the Constitution, it would have been a major setback for gay rights. Thankfully Swiss voters prevented that from happening."

CHAPTER 9

The Swiss Are
Crooked Bankers

As the world's largest international wealth management centre, Switzerland is synonymous with banking. We are not talking about car loans and the paying of utility bills: Switzerland is the global leader in off-shore wealth management. More than one fifth of all the assets held by the world's wealthy individuals outside the borders of their own countries is held in Switzerland, worth a total of USD 2 trillion, according to the Deloitte Wealth Management Centre Ranking (other estimates put the figure higher). The United Kingdom and the United States are next in line for this business with USD 1.7 trillion and USD 1.4 trillion, respectively.

With Switzerland's 261 banks handling colossal amounts of money year after year, there is a widely-held belief, kept alive by both fact and fiction, that this business is being managed dishonestly. The popular image of the Swiss banker as an amoral figure willing to turn a blind eye to the dirty sources of the money he handles has become one of the chief Swiss stereotypes. But is this a fair and accurate representation? That is the two-trillion-dollar question.

What is the attraction of the Swiss financial centre? As an anti-corruption campaigner once pointed out to me, the appeal is the same whether you're straight or crooked. Switzerland, even with banking secrecy actively being dismantled, has a solid reputation for discretion, underscored until recently by its special stance on tax evasion versus tax fraud. Secondly, because of its highly developed banking culture, Switzerland has the money management expertise needed by these people. But equally important, Switzerland is a stable country. Even its currency is a safe haven. Whatever else happens in the world, even war in Europe as we're seeing now in Ukraine, Switzerland will remain safe, stable and secure. That is the guarantee, as much as anything can be guaranteed in life – and it is exactly what criminals and despots want as much as legitimate business people.

There is money to be made from the rich, a fact the Swiss discovered a long time ago. Switzerland's oldest bank at the time of its demise in 2013, Wegelin, was founded in 1741. The bank closed down in disgrace in 2013 after pleading guilty in a New York court to conspiring with American citizens to evade taxes. Wegelin may be gone but a small number of Swiss private banks founded in the era of quill pens and powdered wigs still survive and are thriving. The mantle of Switzerland's oldest bank has been passed on to Landolt & Cie of Lausanne, founded in 1780, though Zurich-based Rahn & Bodmer traces its roots back to 1750 when it began life as a silk trading company that also traded securities, before the banking business was split off. Many historic European banking houses had their origins in trading houses.

The nineteenth century saw Switzerland's neutral status fully recognised at last by the European powers, as well as a tourist boom that attracted the moneyed classes of Europe and the Americas. Even Queen Victoria took a break from conquering the world to sample the delights of the Swiss countryside in 1868. Luxury hotels and tourist railways sprang up to pamper the well-heeled visitors, many drawn by the reputation of the country's mountain spas and sanatoria. Swiss finishing schools like Brilliantmont and Chateau Mont-Choisi, catering for the daughters of the aristocracy and the super-rich, became world famous. In that early phase of tourism Switzerland carved out its niche as a place apart in Europe and it has never lost that cachet. During the twentieth century, Switzerland's immunity from two world wars and the Cold War, coupled with its secure currency and banking secrecy, saw it quickly overtake other European pretenders for the prize of offshore financial kingpin of Europe.

The range of services provided by the Swiss has grown to the point that the country has become a one-stop shop for the super-rich. Here they can have a consultation with their private banker, store gold or art, holiday in exclusive resorts, buy luxury goods, visit their children in boarding school, and attend health clinics. Reputed to be the world's most expensive hotel room, at more than 70,000 francs per night, the 1,700 square-metre royal penthouse suite at the President Wilson hotel in Geneva boasts magnificent views of the lake. In cooler weather guests can also enjoy the view through bullet-proof glass while playing the Steinway grand piano and deciding which of the suite's 12 marble bathrooms to use.

Even the Swiss tax system welcomes rich foreign residents who are permitted to calculate their taxes not on the basis of worldwide income and wealth, but based on annual expenditure, up to a maximum of seven times their annual rent (or what their residence would theoretically cost to rent). Known as lump-sum taxation, this model is only available to non-Swiss citizens who do not work in Switzerland. Living expenses include money spent on housing, dependents, employees, expensive animals like horses, and travel and transport items, including yachts and planes, and must reach a minimum of 400,000 francs. Some cantons, including Zurich and Basel

City have done away with this tax exception. But voters rejected a popular initiative in 2012 calling for lump-sum taxation to be abolished nationwide.

Nevertheless, the Swiss cannot be described as a nation of bankers, any more than they are a nation of hoteliers. Banking provides 165,000 jobs in Switzerland (of which 28,000 work in asset management for customers abroad), or 3.4% of total employment levels. There are multiples more people working in the energy, health, and manufacturing sectors, for example. The Swiss economy has a wide base – the top three exports being gold, packaged medication, and vaccines, followed by watches. However, the banking sector punches above its weight in terms of its wider contribution to the economy and labour productivity. Combined with the insurance sector, the banking sector contributes 13% to the total economy, in directly measurable economic effects, and indirectly, in demand for goods and services in other sectors. Most of this (8% of the 13%) comes from banking (6% direct and 2% indirect).

From crisis to catastrophe
So where does the infamous Swiss banking secrecy fit in here? The law underpinning banking secrecy came into force in Switzerland in 1935 at a time of crisis in the Swiss banking sector when banks were struggling to stay solvent in a difficult European economic climate. Before then it had existed de facto as "an unwritten code of confidentiality similar to the one offered by lawyers, doctors or priests", Robert U. Vogler writes in his book *Swiss Banking Secrecy: Origins, Significance, Myth*. Despite security worries about French and German officials spying on their citizens who were trying to evade heavy post-war taxes, the secrecy issue was not the main focus of the Banking Law of 1934/35. That law was chiefly intended to impose some control on a shaky sector and to reassure the public

by guaranteeing deposits. The banking lobby was strongly opposed to any notion of state regulation, until catastrophe struck in December 1933. The government had to intervene to save the *Schweizer Volksbank* (SVB) with a 100-million-franc bailout, equivalent to almost a quarter of the federal budget for the year. (Not only did banking secrecy start with a bailout, it also ended with one – the Swiss National Bank's 60-billion-franc rescue package for UBS in 2008.)

Banking secrecy was dealt with in Article 47 of 56 articles in the 1934 Banking Law. It decreed that bank employees who divulged confidential information to third parties, whether private persons or government authorities, would be subject to a prison term of up to six months and a fine.

The extent of the banker's obligation to maintain secrecy was not explicitly defined in Article 47, but court rulings established that banks were not permitted to disclose client information to third parties, unless by legal order. Banking secrecy has always been lifted in criminal proceedings but, critically for a significant part of the cross-border business that Swiss banks went on to attract, tax evasion (non-reporting of taxable income) is not a criminal offence in Switzerland. The distinction between tax evasion and tax fraud is important. Let's say you have your savings divided between three bank accounts, but you only report two to the tax authorities. In Switzerland, that transgression, if it ever came to light, would be punished with a fine or penalty taxes. If, however, you reported the three accounts, but provided a falsified document which understated the amount in one of the accounts, that would be fraud and prosecutable. Only then would it be possible for the Swiss authorities to provide legal assistance to foreign tax authorities. This provided a cover for foreign tax cheats to hide behind.

This legal formula stayed in place until 2009, when the distinction was scrapped for foreign clients of Swiss banks in a bid

Switzerland's most famous cartoonist, Chappatte, has produced a series of cartoons on banking secrecy

to limit tax evasion. The death knell for Swiss banking secrecy came in 2010 when Swiss parliament endorsed a deal with the US to hand over data on 4,450 UBS account holders suspected of tax evasion. Throughout this period, the rest of the world (as represented by the 34-member Organisation for Economic Cooperation and Development, OECD), hungry for tax revenue after the financial crisis, was putting serious pressure on the Swiss and others to comply with more stringent international transparency standards. Tax evasion, which had been tolerated if not practiced by the political class for decades, was suddenly out of fashion.

Now that Switzerland has signed up to the new world banking norm of the "automatic exchange of information" which comes into force in 2018, Swiss banking secrecy for customers beyond its borders can truly be said to be over. From then on Swiss banks will deliver information on account holders and accounts to the Swiss tax authorities, which will then exchange information with the tax authorities in other participating countries. But there is a weakness in this new model, which has been pointed out by anti-corruption campaigners, like Public Eye. Automatic exchange might not benefit developing countries in real terms because the OECD stipulates it has to be a two-way street. A country can only obtain automatically exchanged information if it is able to transmit similar data itself, but the necessary technical and administrative infrastructure is still lacking in many developing countries. Holders of illegal fortunes may continue to be welcome customers.

The scrapping of banking secrecy is a bitter pill for many Swiss citizens and not a change they want to see introduced at home. Respect for financial privacy is paramount in Switzerland under a self-assessed tax system that assumes honest accounting. In conversation, a Swiss economics professor once put it this way: "The Swiss have a split personality when it comes to banking. On the one hand they believe in following rules and the importance of trust, on the other hand they are defensive of a system that attracted and served the worst kinds of rule breakers."

The Swiss electorate will ultimately have the final say on whether banks will also automatically pass on their data to the Swiss tax office, when they vote on the "protection of the private sphere" initiative, which aims to give domestic banking secrecy constitutional protection.

Ain't misbehaving
Defenders of Swiss banking secrecy used to argue that the legislation was enacted to protect legal behaviour from illegitimate investigation and was never intended to protect illegal behaviour from legitimate investigation. But it hasn't always looked that way.

When you consider the recent scandals involving Petrobras (300 accounts at more than 30 Swiss banking institutions holding USD 400 million that were apparently used to process bribery payments under investigation in Brazil), FIFA (USD 80 million frozen in 13 bank accounts relating the corruption investigation of football's world governing body), the former Russian minister for agriculture Elena Skrynnik (funds frozen in Switzerland as part of a Swiss money-laundering investigation; Russian media reporting USD 140 million fraud) – by far not an exhaustive list – it cannot be denied that there is tainted money sloshing around in Swiss banks.

On the other side of the balance sheet, the Swiss are highly active in freezing and repatriating illegally procured funds, having developed robust legislation for this purpose. Swiss banking culture has changed beyond recognition since the 1980s and the first know-your-customer agreement of 1987. Federal laws, the financial regulator, the banks' representative body and internal compliance departments all set very high standards for compliance. In short, there are probably more Swiss people occupied with combatting money laundering than facilitating it.

When we talk about dodgy money, it is important to point out that there are different categories of shady customers, arguably located at different points in the immorality spectrum. Let's classify them as different types of hamburgers on the menu of nastiness to make things easier – and more fun.

The Crimi-burger

First of all, you have the money flowing from organised crime like drug dealing, forced prostitution or gun running. The triple decker greasy Crimi-burger is made with E. coli contaminated meat and served with all the trimmings and extra sides. Mafia groups have been known to use Swiss-based intermediaries to launder money. In 2003 for example, a Ticino-based lawyer, Francesco Moretti, was found guilty of laundering 60 million francs as part of a massive Mafia-run cocaine deal. The authorities seized 12 million francs in cash from a cupboard in his office while he was away in Mexico. Despite a plea for leniency by Moretti's lawyer, who argued that his client was a fly trapped in the spider's web of organised crime, the court sentenced the 63-year-old to 14 years in prison. Simply nasty.

The Klepto-burger

The next supersize category features the crooked political elite from countries where being connected to the regime is a licence to steal money. The Klepto-burger is just as sickening as the Crimi-burger, but is enriched with fat-cat sauce, enhanced with flavours of violence. Untold millions were kept in abject poverty to make this meal. The most infamous names from this group – Sani Abacha of Nigeria who transferred at least USD 800 million to Swiss banks, Ferdinand Marcos who was president of the Philippines from 1965 to 1986 (USD 683 million eventually returned to the country from Swiss accounts), Jean-Claude "Baby Doc" Duvalier of Haiti (accused of embezzling USD 540 million of state funds) – are a throwback from the bad old days before anyone thought of using the words ethical and finance together. The more recent names, such as the pre-Arab Spring leaders, Ben Ali of Tunisia (60 million francs blocked in Swiss banks) and Egypt's Mubarak (700 million francs frozen in Switzerland), seemed untouchable when they were in power. The brazen pocket lining extends to the entourage too. Forty-eight people are named on Switzerland's list of frozen assets in the Ben Ali case alone. The criminal and political cases come to light partly due to proactive work on the part of banks, prosecutors and campaigners, and partly as a fallout from regime changes.

The Sly-burger

Our third sandwich looks just fine – crisp vegetables and a toasted bun. But bite in and you'll see this isn't wholesome meat. Here we have the common-or-garden variety rich person who wants part of their assets kept off the radar at home, for tax purposes. This burger might have been specially made by one of the Swiss banks who were gleefully recruiting in the United States until the US Department of Justice (DoJ) landed on them like a ton of bricks.

Swiss wrongdoing in the US came to light when former UBS employee Bradley Birkenfeld turned whistle-blower in 2007, approaching the DoJ with evidence of systematic assisted tax evasion within the bank. Criminal proceedings followed and UBS settled in 2009 with a USD 780-million fine. An American citizen, Birkenfeld served two and a half years for aiding and abetting tax fraud but on his release received USD 104 million, less taxes, from the US Treasury as his whistle-blower's cut.

UBS was one of many Swiss banks courting rich American clients with special arrangements. Credit Suisse, also pursued by the DoJ, was forced to pay a fine of USD 2.8 billion in 2014. A further 80 Swiss banks came forward as part of an amnesty brokered between the Swiss Federal Department of Finance and the DoJ in 2013, owning up to their wrongdoing and paying fines – totalling USD 1.4 billion. That deal, the Swiss Bank Program, was only open to banks not already under criminal investigation. Swiss banks were found to have used all sorts of tricks to keep their clients' money hidden. Some issued hard-to-trace debit cards without the client's name on them. There were also various ways of disguising the owner of assets, through insurance policies or sham entities. Another practice was to break large cash transfers down into multiple small amounts under USD 10,000 to avoid the scrutiny of the US tax authorities.

Banks held on to post so that no incriminating letters would be in circulation, and there were code phrases for withdrawals, like: "Can you download some tunes for us?" The secret agent behaviour got out of hand in a pressurised environment. Birkenfeld himself admitted to smuggling diamonds for a client inside a tube of toothpaste. All in all, a damning indictment of an "anything goes" culture protected by banking secrecy.

The Pro-burger

On special offer you have the Sly-burger Lite, also known as the Pro-burger. Bite-size, economical, and easy to hide. Those who consume these burgers are professionals from neighbouring countries in particular, those German dentists and Italian architects who like to keep a Swiss account. You will be hungry again an hour after eating this panini-style snack. Famous samplers include French minister Jérôme Cahuzac, who was forced to resign in 2013 when it was discovered he had undeclared money in Swiss accounts.

The existence of many of these burgers came to light through data leaks. The biggest leak in banking history occurred when an employee of HSBC in Geneva took advantage of his access to the bank's database to steal data on some 130,000 of the bank's clients. Hervé Falciani, a French-Italian citizen, handed the information over to the French authorities in 2008 and it was subsequently passed on to several European governments. In November 2015 Falciani was sentenced in absentia to five years in prison by the Swiss federal criminal court. Also in 2015, HSBC was fined 40 million francs by a Geneva court for allowing money laundering to take place at its Swiss subsidiary due to "organisational deficiencies".

Stolen data was all the rage in recent years, and some former banking staff made a killing from their breach of trust. German IT worker Lutz Otte told the *Wall Street Journal* that he didn't regret stealing client data from his employer, Zurich-based Julius Baer Group, in 2011. He made more than 600,000 euros by selling the profiles of 2,700 German clients to German tax authorities through a middleman in Berlin. Otte was caught in 2012 and served a year in prison. Now he lives in northern Germany and hints in newspaper interviews that he has more data to sell, identifying clients of other nationalities. Scandals such as these are effective in forcing tax cheats out of the woodwork. Between 2010 and 2014, the German state of North Rhine-Wesphalia bought several CDs containing stolen data of German citizens' accounts in Swiss banks. During that period almost 19,000 tax evaders in that state alone voluntarily owned up to the authorities.

This latter category of tax-shy customer is set to become a historical one, at least in Switzerland, amid rapidly advancing international cooperation on the cross-border exchange of banking information. Meanwhile, those in possession of substantial fortunes will continue to find ways of reducing their tax bill to modest levels using legitimate tax avoidance schemes and impenetrable illegal ones.

The Banker
Ultra-high-net worth individuals, with assets of more than USD 100 million, are the dream clients for Swiss private bankers, as I discovered when I went to meet a private banker in Geneva for a chat.

What does a banker for ultra-high-net worth individuals look like? First you have to find his lair. I wander down the stretch of street that matches the address, unable to find the bank. Even the staff in the corner café 20 metres away have never heard of the place. This is what's known as discretion. Retracing my steps, I finally spot the bank's plaque on the wall and slip into the entrance lobby of the right building.

Minutes later I am waiting in a cream-coloured room on one side of a large table when the man I have come to interview appears, exuding gravitas and goodwill. He has the air of someone who became middle-aged very young and will remain in this age bracket for an implausibly long time. There is a priest-like solemnity in how he pours my coffee from a silver tea pot. I could tell him my sins.

A recent scandal – there is always a recent scandal in Swiss banking – provides a good starting point for our discussion. He shakes his head sadly. "The rogue element, this tiny minority of rule breakers, tarnish the reputation of Swiss banking and are not representative of the industry. Why do it? There is no need to court questionable clients, absolutely no need when there is plenty of reputable business out there and clear due diligence procedures to follow."

Curious to know more about the super-rich, I ask the banker to give me a general overview of his clientele. They include traditional businessmen who've built manufacturing empires, the new tycoons of the emerging economies, young people who've inherited their millions – and, always, those members of the ruling elite from countries that have a loose relationship with the rule of law, known in the business as politically exposed persons or PEPs.

We get onto the subject of dictators' assets, also known as potentate funds, which are an important development policy issue. The World Bank estimates that the channelling of potentate funds from developing countries to foreign financial centres causes losses of between 20 billion and 40 billion dollars every year. That's up to 40% of the money received in development aid by those countries.

My banker gives an ecclesiastical shrug, and then adds:

Don't forget, before these leaders are toppled, they are afforded the same level of respect on the global stage as

Chappatte makes his point

democratic leaders. One day you see them on TV being wined and dined in the Elysée Palace, the next minute they are behind bars and their mansions are being trashed by the mob. We bankers can only operate within the status quo. We cannot introduce our own sanctions where no political sanctions exist. I have clients connected to undemocratic regimes in the Middle East and sometimes I wonder how long they can hold onto their positions of power. In the meantime, I am here to do business.

Two years after I met my friendly banker, his bank was involved in a scandal with a politically exposed client who had hundreds of millions of dollars to play with. I wonder how the few-bad-apples defence is holding up now.

The assumption that Swiss banks play a big part in hiding this money raises hackles in Swiss officialdom because the

Swiss do far more than any other country to repatriate illicit funds, having developed some of the world's most advanced legislation in this area.

Over the last 20 years Switzerland has successfully returned approximately USD 1.8 billion of potentate funds to their countries of origin. Swiss willingness to freeze and repatriate ill-gotten gains is markedly higher than that shown by other financial centres. As far back as 1986, funds connected to Ferdinand Marcos were frozen within hours of his removal from power. Some USD 650 million in stolen funds were eventually returned to the country. Has this record of freezing accounts turned new tainted business away? Not all of it, judging by the scandals that are still coming to light. Certain clients have a life history that makes them feel untouchable. Besides, they are prestige junkies, and what could be more prestigious than having a Swiss banker waiting on you hand and foot?

But the message from the top is clear: "Switzerland has a fundamental interest in ensuring that no illicit assets of politically exposed persons (PEPs) – so-called potentate funds – enter its financial centre," the Federal Department of Foreign Affairs states on its website.

Suspicious minds

As for illegally acquired funds in Swiss banks today, there are mechanisms in place to deal with cases when they arise. When banks suspect that the client they are dealing with may have procured assets illegally, they are supposed to freeze the account, fill out a "suspicious activity report" and send it to the Money Laundering Reporting Office in Bern. This happened about 2,900 times in 2016. That's a lot of suspicious activity. Most of these reports were forwarded to the prosecution authorities, representing 2.5 billion francs in suspicious assets.

This all sounds good. But as a share of the total amount of assets on the balance sheet of Swiss banks it's a drop in the ocean. Interestingly, three quarters of the cases referred to prosecutors are suspended or dismissed, often because it is impossible to get hard evidence from other countries.

These are the channels for banks doing their own policing. Where bankers want to cheat or turn a blind eye, it's difficult to see through closed doors. Unless you are the Swiss Financial Market Supervisory Authority, Finma. Stringent due diligence (background checking) and reporting requirements are laid down by the law, and Finma is tasked with ensuring compliance. In severe cases, Finma may impose measures to restore compliance with the law, organise extraordinary audits and confiscate profits. But you won't hear about it, at least not directly. Finma only recently broke its code of confidentiality and decided to start publishing an enforcement report with anonymised case summaries once a year.

The Office of the Attorney General is another crusader against wrongdoing in the financial sector. Sometimes it acts on the basis of complaints sent by outside parties, such as the London-based campaigners for justice for Sergei Magnitsky, who was wrongly arrested and killed in custody in Moscow, or the Swiss-based Bruno Manser Fund which campaigns for the rights of indigenous people in Indonesia. Sometimes, as in the Petrobras case, the scams are massive.

But even when we're not talking about bribery and corruption, managing the wealth of billionaires, even those who operate above board, raises its own moral questions. I asked my friendly banker if he could sleep at night knowing his role is to safeguard obscene amounts of money concentrated in the hands of so few. "I sleep fine," he tells me earnestly. "The money is there and needs to be managed. It cannot be wished away."

And then he tells me how difficult it is for the vastly rich, the pressure they live under:

> The biggest worry they have is about their children's future. Protect them too little and they could be prey to gold-digging relationships; protect too much and you are creating a gilded cage. These are the kinds of things we talk about. Especially the older generation, who have accumulated so much wealth that their children need never work. Apart from their personal doctor and private banker, who else can they trust?

If you ain't cheating, you ain't trying

Swiss banks have been found to be involved in so many different spheres of wrongdoing, it is difficult not to lose faith in the entire sector. In May 2015, UBS pleaded guilty to wire fraud and agreed to pay USD $545 million to settle cases of market manipulation in the US. The case, in which five other global banks were fined, involved the manipulation of foreign exchange rates and of the Libor (London Interbank Offered Rate) interest rate. According to Reuters, employees of the banks were using invitation-only chat rooms and coded language to coordinate their trades. One of the group, admittedly not Swiss, was quoted from the transcripts as saying, "If you ain't cheating, you ain't trying".

A few months later, the Swiss competition authority began an investigation into the potential manipulation of prices in the trading of precious metals involving two Swiss banks, UBS and Julius Baer, and five others. The seven banks are suspected of rigging the spreads (the difference between bid and offer prices) on metals such as gold, silver and platinum.

And then, in April 2016, came the Panama Papers, which uncovered a world of double dealing and unethical financial practices facilitated by the Panamanian law firm Mossack

Fonseca, in which Swiss banks played a prominent role. A huge leak of more than 11 million Mossack Fonseca documents – emails, bank accounts and client records – obtained by the International Consortium of Investigative Journalists (ICIJ), revealed the inner workings of the company which provided hundreds of thousands of offshore holdings to individuals and firms from more than 200 countries.

Mossack Fonseca is described by the ICIJ as one of the world's five largest wholesalers of offshore secrecy. It has helped spread an invisible cloak over the assets of thousands of wealthy clients. Until 2011, the number three in the company was a Swiss man, Christoph Zollinger. And of the 10 financial institutions requesting the most offshore companies for clients, four are Swiss. Switzerland ranked high in terms of both the number (1,200) and activity level (second highest) of intermediaries.

> They [the documents] recount example after example of ethical and legal wrongdoing by clients," the ICIJ wrote, "and provide evidence of a firm happy to act as a gatekeeper to the secrets of its clients, even those who turn out to be crooks, members of the Mafia, drug dealers, corrupt politicians and tax evaders.

Mossack Fonseca has three offices in Switzerland. But they are not the only Panamanian firm setting up letterbox companies in Panama for the customers of Swiss financial institutions. The Morgan & Morgan Group, which offers legal, trust and financial services, has had a Swiss subsidiary in Zurich since 1980 called MMG Panazur, which describes itself as "one of Europe's leading providers of corporate services from different jurisdictions".

The Swiss *Sonntagsblick* newspaper reported that UBS bank employees helped their clients hide money from the tax authorities through Panama companies for years. The newspaper quoted a former UBS banker: "My UBS team bought hundreds, if not thousands, of letterbox companies in Panama for clients. Definitely 90% of clients were using this to conceal funds from the tax authorities." MMG Panazur charged 1,000 francs to open a Panama company, while bankers billed clients up to 4,000 francs for acting as a middleman.

Writing in the Swiss financial news portal *finews.ch*, David Zollinger, a specialist in commercial criminal law who formerly handled money laundering cases for the Zurich public prosecutor, said the problem lies with the people on the frontline and their superiors:

> To be clear: The problem with PEPs is by no means a problem of recognition, but the question about the source of their wealth. If anyone is wondering where the implementation emergency is, this is where to look. My experience (as a public prosecutor, senior bank employee and as an advisor) has shown that employees of financial intermediaries usually know very well which boxes have to be ticked where on the form. They also know what is expected of them with regard to a client profile. But what neither they nor often their superiors know is how to ask the client the questions that are really relevant, and how to react when they don't get the answers they actually need.

Short of introducing a totalitarian surveillance society, Zollinger did not believe there was a quick fix to the problem of financial intermediaries turning a blind eye. Tough sanctions don't help unless there is a high chance of getting caught. More regulation means just more form filling. It is too early to say if the pressure coming from public opinion will bring about any meaningful change.

Treasure trove

The strong banking tradition helped the Swiss build up trust for the storage of all sorts of valuables. Where does the Picasso family keep their art collection? In Geneva. To be more specific, in an industrial zone in La Praille a few kilometres from Geneva city centre where the Geneva Freeport is located. If you are not fabulously wealthy or working in the art business, you won't be familiar with the concept of a free port. Also called a bonded warehouse, this is a secure place where valuable goods can be stored, incurring no tax until they are removed from the premises, even if they are sold. The system dates back to the early nineteenth century, when warehouses were set up to help with the management of imported goods between arrival in a port and sale. Many countries still operate free ports of varying sizes and the Geneva site has developed a lucrative niche catering for the international fine art trade. The Geneva premises is run by the limited company *Ports Francs et Entrepôts de Genève*, whose majority shareholder is the Canton of Geneva. It houses quantities of artworks, gold and collectibles such as wine, jewellery, cigars and cars. Concerned that the free port could be used for smuggling or money-laundering purposes, Switzerland changed the law in 2007 to bring the ports under the control of Swiss customs. Swiss customs officers now keep a record of what goes in and out, but this information is not made public.

More than half of the internationally traded art in auction houses and direct sales goes through Geneva Freeport, according to some estimates. That means more art has passed through La Praille than is visible in all the world's great museums put together, 1.2 million pieces were stored there at last count. This is a world within a world where art is bought as an investment and requires expensive long-term storage facilities. Lots of museums store art there for tax reasons. Paintings change hands without ever leaving the premises. Owners are only obliged to pay transaction tax and customs duty when they take the artwork out.

Never mind the free port, there is another way to store valuables in Switzerland without the contents appearing on any kind of inventory – a safe deposit box. You may think of a safe deposit box as a container the size of a desk drawer but you can rent a "safe deposit box" the size of a room. One thing you would definitely find in these boxes, if you were ever allowed to look, is cash. By value, 60% of Swiss bank notes in circulation are in 1,000 franc notes, worth a total of 38 billion francs. As the UBS whistle-blower Bradley Birkenfeld said in a 2015 CNBC interview: "I mean, you could put a half a million dollars in your pocket, no problem." The Swiss National Bank has acknowledged that "the high proportion of large denominations indicates that the banknotes are used not only as a means of payment but also – to a considerable degree – as a store of value". British government advisor and former top banker Peter Sands put it more bluntly in his paper calling for the scrapping of large denomination notes, observing that they "play little role in the functioning of the legitimate economy [and] a crucial role in the underground economy". The European Central Bank recently announced it would scrap the 500 euro note for exactly this reason – but not the Swiss. Perhaps we'll see a lot of this cash come out of the woodwork when the new series of Swiss bank notes is fully rolled out by the end of 2019 and the old banknotes are withdrawn.

Not only is Switzerland an art hub and a banking hub, it is also the epicentre of the world's gold trade: four of the biggest gold refineries are based in Switzerland, refining two-thirds of the world's raw gold. Three of the big four are located in the southern canton of Ticino, as Italy was historically one of the leading producers of gold jewellery. For example, Pamp of Castel San Pietro, which produces a complete range of precious metal bars in all shapes, purities and sizes, has an annual refining capacity of 450 tons. Global mine production of gold in 2016 was 3,100 metric tons, and the biggest gold refinery in Switzerland, Valcambi of Balerna, has an annual refining capacity of more than half that, about 1,600 tons. The Swiss government withheld the data breakdown on precious metals imports and exports for decades, only opening up in 2014 with the overall figures, and in 2015 with the amounts per country. The optimist in me would like to read this as another positive sign that the Swiss establishment is prepared to relax its traditional code of confidentiality in the interests of transparency.

Caught up in a seemingly constant round of bad publicity since the financial crisis of 2008, Swiss banking has suffered some serious blows to its reputation. When the sub-prime scandal brought UBS close to ruin, Swiss bankers appeared to be lacking in wisdom. When bankers were found to be playing unethical games in the US to help tax cheats, they lost dignity. It was impossible to claim the moral high ground when CDs of stolen client data started circulating in neighbouring countries, or when the OECD put Switzerland on a grey list of non tax-compliant countries. In a very humbling process, the Swiss have had to admit to their faults and compromise on secrecy, changing the law and releasing the names of banking clients to please the US, as well as signing a dozen double taxation agreements in six months to please the OECD. Now they have to adapt to the new reality created by these legal changes.

These challenges have shaken the sector but have not produced any kind of great unravelling. Between 2008 and 2014, Swiss banks lost 7% of client assets but still ended up with growth, thanks to positive market performance during this recovery period, Deloitte revealed in its latest wealth management centre report. The playing field has changed, but the Swiss financial centre is here to stay, as Patrick Odier, then chairman of the Swiss Bankers Association, told a banking audience on Bankers' Day in September 2015. His speech echoed Cathy describing her love for Heathcliff in *Wuthering Heights* as "a source of little visible delight, but necessary":

> Over the past few years, we have had a tendency to forget the importance of the financial centre. The banking sector was often criticised, sometimes for reasons that were understandable, other times for ideological reasons, but whether we like it or not, the financial centre is to the Swiss economy what oxygen is to the human body: necessary for existence.

CHAPTER 10

The Swiss Have the World's Best Democracy

When a school board in the bilingual town of Biel/Bienne knowingly hired a teacher who had served a sentence for child sexual abuse, they had no idea that their decision would ultimately lead to a change in the national law. A local parents' group that had previously campaigned on child protection issues, *Marche Blanche* (White March), heard about the man's appointment and swiftly organised a protest and a petition calling for his removal. But the board refused to reverse its decision, saying the teacher had been the best candidate for the job. There was no legal basis for barring him from working with children.

That was in 2004. Local representatives got involved in the case, raising the issue of tougher sanctions for paedophiles in federal parliament but they failed to get their colleagues interested. *Marche Blanche* was not prepared to let the issue drop. They believed convicted paedophiles, without exception, should be banned for life from working with children, and they thought voters would agree with them. Unlike grassroots campaigners in most other democracies, this group had a political tool at their disposal – the popular initiative. This tool makes it possible for campaigners to write their own dream law and, if they can collect enough signatures, force a nationwide vote on it.

The campaigners joined forces with other like-minded groups and gathered more than 100,000 signatures around the country within the prescribed timeframe of 18 months. Clipboard-wielding signature hunters are a common sight on Swiss streets. The *Marche Blanche* signatures were delivered to the Federal Chancellery in Bern in 2011.

A popular vote was scheduled for May 2014. Slow to reach agreement, parliament finalised its own alternative version of tougher sanctions for paedophiles in November 2013, and the government asked voters to allow this solution be implemented instead of accepting the *Marche Blanche* proposal. The alternative sanctions allowed for fixed-term bans on working with children, which could be extended by judges. But *Marche Blanche* stuck to its guns, insisting that the lifetime-ban on working with children should be imposed in every case. In the end 63.5% of voters agreed with them, going against the will of their government and parliament.

There is no matching the power of the Swiss people within their political system of direct democracy combined with parliamentary democracy. Simply put, direct democracy is about citizens having more decision-making power than their elected representatives. Unlike the electorate in regular parliamentary democracies, whose influence evaporates once deputies have taken their seats, Swiss voters retain their leverage. They can also block new laws: if at least 50,000 signatures are collected within 100 days of the official publication of the proposed legislation, a referendum is held. Voters are also called upon to approve any changes to the Constitution or when Switzerland wants to join an international organisation, such as the United Nations, a step voters first rejected, in 1986, and then approved in 2002.

The direct democracy system is not only practiced on a federal level but on a cantonal and communal level. A commune can be as small as a village of a few dozen souls or as big as a city. Four out of five communes still make direct democratic decisions at the communal assembly, where all inhabitants who are entitled to vote may participate. Appenzell Innerrhoden is the smallest canton by population with some 16,000 residents, while Zurich, with a population of 1.5 million, has the biggest headcount. True to federalist principles, the smaller cantons punch above their weight in people's initiatives, thanks to the double majority provision; all people's initiatives need to be accepted by a majority of cantons, as well as a simple majority of votes.

Anything from the right to assisted suicide, to new architectural projects, to changes in the tax regime can be proposed or challenged by voters. Under the voter-driven system of popular initiatives and referendums, all sorts of changes have been approved or forced through in recent years – a plan to phase out nuclear power, the construction of new Alpine railways, a ban on the construction of minarets, and various immigration restrictions.

Some of the initiatives or new laws that have been rejected include a proposal to scrap the army, one to introduce a minimum wage, easier naturalisation for second and third-generation foreigners, and a proposal to oblige the Swiss National Bank to hold 20% of its assets in gold.

The federal and cantonal votes are grouped together and held on Sundays four times throughout the year. The results of initiatives and referendums in Switzerland are made public that same day, not necessarily because the Swiss count faster than the rest of us (they might), but because the majority of people have already voted in advance by post. Polling stations are opened in every community on voting Sundays but they are only attended by a handful of people. For most people, voting is not a social event any more, it is a solitary activity, carried

Brochures from all the political parties arrive in one envelope

out in a quiet moment at home. In this way Swiss voters enjoy a kitchen table democracy.

There's a lot to admire in the Swiss democratic system: one house of parliament, the National Council, has 200 members who are chosen through proportional representation. The second chamber, the Council of States, has equal representation from each of the 20 cantons (two seats each) and one seat from each of the six half cantons (see glossary). The cantons have their own legislature, constitution and courts. All these public representatives are kept on a short leash by people power. The Swiss government is the seven-member Federal Council, the seven cabinet posts shared between the four main political parties, with ministers taking turns in the role of president. Consensus is the order of the day – in official matters, the Federal Council always speaks with one voice.

Yet all is not well in the Confederation. Voter turnout is low, there is a lack of transparency in political party funding, and behind-the-scenes lobbying is rampant. A raft of recent popular initiatives has put lawmakers in a position where they are practically forced to introduce measures that scupper international agreements, contravene human rights or are unconstitutional. Swiss democracy: running riot or running out of steam?

Close to the people

Sitting at a table in the corner of the train station café in Fribourg was the man I had come to meet. To my surprise, he had suggested a rendezvous at the station because he was due to pass through Fribourg on his way back from Bern to his home town of Martigny. I walked up to former President Pascal Couchepin, quite possibly the tallest person to hold the office, and said hello. We proceeded to have an interesting discussion about Swiss foreign policy, democracy and society (see Chapter 6, In focus) while the other patrons of the café stole discreet glances at our table.

I shouldn't have been surprised that a former Swiss president would be travelling around the country solo by public transport. A year earlier the then-president Didier Burkhalter was photographed on the platform of Neuchâtel station casually waiting with other commuters for his train, an image that caused much bemusement on Twitter. A colleague of mine claims he was almost knocked down in Bern by another former president on a bicycle – Moritz Leuenberger.

The culture of accessibility around Swiss politics is exceptional. The fear of the mob that exists in many other countries is absent, which means no gates and guards keeping the public at a distance from government buildings. The open space in front of the parliament building in Bern, the *Bundesplatz / Place Fédérale / Piazza Federale*, was used as a car park for many years. When it was decided to redevelop the square for the new millennium, the architects were given the brief to make the

The gold vaults of the Swiss National Bank are reputed to lie below the Bundesplatz

space *volksnah*, "near to the people", an abiding principle of the Swiss political system.

The square was paved with metamorphic stone quarried from Vals in eastern Switzerland and fitted with jet fountains embedded under the surface, leaving a flat open space. The *Bundesplatz* is now a multi-purpose city square, used for a twice weekly farmers' market and many other gatherings. On hot days, children play in the water jets; in the winter the authorities set up an ice rink. Throughout the year, the square is open for concerts and demonstrations.

At the inauguration of the new square on Swiss National Day in 2004, the president of the year Joseph Deiss said the new *Bundesplatz* was a model for Swiss politics. "Its emptiness allows for openness in thinking ... Which our politicians need as well. Let's use it as a metaphor for a new Switzerland, for a country reaching out to the world."

Thanks to its annual rotating presidency, Switzerland is awash with former presidents, few of them rising to international prominence. The whole point is that no single person should ever stand for Switzerland. In the railway café, Couchepin recalled a conversation he once had with an interpreter on a trip to Russia. "The interpreter said to me, it is a happy country where we don't know the president."

In Switzerland, the most important voice is the voice of the people – *das Volk*. Any politician who wants to silence his or her opponent need only say the magic words, "the people have decided", and the discussion is strangled. This ingrained respect for the people's will, as expressed by voters, appears noble. But has it opened the door to a distorted kind of democracy – a tyranny of the majority, where the rights of minorities are no longer safeguarded?

Some observers fear this is the case, among them Philippe Mastronardi, professor of public law at St Gallen University. He was one of the experts featured in a 2015 documentary about Swiss democracy made by Thomas Isler, *Die Demokratie ist los* (Democracy on the Loose). "If you define democracy absolutely as the sovereignty of the people," Mastronardi said, "and say democracy is the absolute rule of the people and no one else has anything to say about it, then you have not grasped what democracy is. Then you believe all the authorities are just cogs in a democracy, and that would be the dictatorship of the majority."

The documentary focuses on three recent successful popular initiatives – the vote to curb immigration of European Union nationals of February 2014, passed by the slimmest majority (50.3%), the 2010 vote to automatically deport foreign criminals (52% in favour), both spearheaded by the Swiss People's Party, and the vote to block the purchase of a new fleet of army jets (53% in favour), put forward by a small but active organisation, Group for Switzerland Without an Army.

Whenever critics point out the shortcomings of direct democracy, the response from the winning side is the same. The argument can be summed up in the words of Swiss People's Party parliamentarian Luzi Stamm, speaking to Isler in a corridor of the parliament building in *Die Demokratie ist los*. Stamm addresses the filmmaker directly. "The Swiss people are the highest legal power. When the Swiss say someone will be deported if he commits a crime, then that is how it is, whether you like it or not."

Minority rule?
So who are Swiss voters? Some 5.2 million Swiss citizens have the right to vote out of a population of eight million. In federal elections and most initiatives, fewer than half of them exercise that right. Two million Swiss residents with foreign citizenship do not have federal voting rights. Out of some 750,000 people with Swiss citizenship who live abroad and have the right to vote, only around 147,000 are registered to vote. In other words, Swiss living abroad can vote, even if they have never lived in Switzerland, while Swiss-born foreigners cannot. When, as often happens, a vote is carried by a narrow margin on a low turnout, the system allows 1.3 million people, for example, to dictate the conditions under which eight million people live. That is *das Volk*. In an echo of what happened with the evolution of women's suffrage, cantons are leading the way in extending voting rights to foreigners. Neuchâtel and Vaud gave women the right to vote in 1959, 12 years before they won the right to vote at federal level. Today, one third of cantons allow long-term foreign residents the right to vote at cantonal or communal level.

Many communes organise an annual celebratory event for 18-year-old citizens, welcoming them to the voting club and showing them how to exercise their democratic rights. But there is no obligation to vote in Switzerland, with the exception of canton Schaffhausen, and more often than not, citizens avail themselves of the freedom not to participate in the political system. The rate of voter participation goes up with age. Pensioners are twice as likely to exercise their right to vote as those in the 18 to 25 age group. Voter turnout for federal parliamentary elections, held every four years, has not risen above 50% since 1979, hopping around between 42% and 49%. Voter turnout for the last parliamentary elections in France was 48.7% but participation reached 77% for the French presidential elections. In the United Kingdom, 66% of voters cast a vote in the 2015 parliamentary elections. Italy, Austria and Germany have a stronger voting culture, still above 70% for parliamentary elections. However, turnout in European Union countries falls dramatically for European elections – below 50% for all of the aforementioned countries, except Italy (57%).

Contributing to the lack of interest in Switzerland is the fact that the system has cut the link between the allocation of votes and the profile of the new government. If voters cannot achieve or prevent a particular outcome, why bother? Power at the top is shared coalition-style, under a deal in place since 1959. The four largest parties share the seven cabinet seats according to their electoral support, traditionally a two, two, two, one breakdown (from 2007 to 2015, five parties shared cabinet posts after a split within the Swiss People's Party). This much-lauded magic formula has given Switzerland unbeatable political stability but it has also taken the urgency out of elections.

"From this perspective, low voter turnout can act as a signal that something is wrong – not with the voters who fail to turn out or with the society of which they are part, but with a political system in which politicians have contrived to make elections less relevant," Mark N. Franklin, author of *Voter Turnout and the Dynamics of Electoral Competition in Established Democracies*, writes, citing the United States and Switzerland as bad examples.

Voter turnout for popular initiatives and referendums has averaged slightly above 40% in recent years, with some notable exceptions, such as the 1989 popular initiative for Switzerland without an army, which spurred 69% of voters to the polls, and the referendum on membership of the European Economic Area, a half-way house to EU membership, which motivated a record 78% of the electorate to vote. Both were rejected. Passion and unpredictability are still very much in evidence in federal votes. A recent clear exception to the low turnout trend was the 63% turnout for the "enforcement initiative" in February 2016. Voters rejected the reworked initiative to automatically expel foreign criminals by 59%, having accepted an earlier version of the proposal in 2009.

Also rejected by the electorate: any attempt to make it easier for foreigners to get Swiss citizenship, and thus swell the ranks of voters. Swiss democracy is evidently too good to share, as this 2008 quote from a Swiss People's Party campaign demonstrates. "Swiss citizenship law is unique. In no other country in the world do citizens have such extensive voting and freedom rights as in Switzerland. That is why the question of who should receive this citizenship is a leading political question."

The issue has flared up again since parliament voted in March 2015 to accept a proposal submitted by Social Democrat Ada Marra to make the naturalisation process easier for the grandchildren of immigrants, while still examining candidates on a case-by-case basis. Some 100,000 people stand to benefit from the reform. But the Swiss People's Party, against any adjustments that could be interpreted as mass naturalisation, has vowed to fight the move at the ballot box again.

In a recent essay in the University of Zurich quarterly *UZH Magazin*, leading historian Jakob Tanner noted that the restrictive side of Swiss democracy has a long history:

> The fiction of democratic equality is combined in Switzerland with a markedly exclusive definition of people's sovereignty. Severe exclusion criteria have always applied, at the end of the nineteenth century against marginalised people, up to 1971 against women, today against the majority of immigrants. In proportion to the population, the "sovereign people" has always been remarkably small. Battles for the extension of participatory and social rights pervade Swiss politics to this day and display an emotionally-loaded dynamic that is anything but boring.

Could do better

Writing in critical terms about direct democracy, two members of the think tank Avenir Suisse came forward in 2015 with a set of reforms which they believe are essential to stop "the most important instrument in Swiss democracy from turning into a farce". Popular initiatives and referendums used to be used sparingly and had a low chance of success. In the 110 years from 1891 to 2001, only 12 out of 145 initiatives were approved. In recent years there has been a glut of nationwide votes, achieving a much higher success rate, but few have been implemented in the full spirit of their initiators. From 2002 to 2015, 10 of 53 passed. Researchers Lukas Rühli and Tibère Adler argue that reform is urgently needed to improve the effectiveness of these votes, while preventing their abuse.

"The referendum [...] has become distanced from its true function as a tool for expressing popular opposition. Its purpose today has turned more into a party political instrument for certain governing parties, or a marketing gambit for the wishes of specific minority interests," the authors claim. Looking at the groups and parties behind current initiatives, it is not clear that any one political grouping has undue influence. The entire political spectrum was represented in the six initiatives voted on in February and June 2016. February saw an initiative on the tax treatment of married couples, brought by the Christian Democrats; the Young Socialists had a proposal to end speculation on foodstuffs; and the Swiss People's Party was back with round two of its deportation campaign. Of the three June initiatives, one was brought by a group representing the car lobby, one came from consumer groups unhappy with cutbacks and the use of profits in public services, and a proposal for unconditional basic income for all was brought by a group of "humanists, artists and entrepreneurs". All six initiatives were rejected by voters.

Nevertheless, Rühli and Tibère say that a situation is developing where voters, assuming that only a watered-down version of a proposal will be implemented, will be more inclined to support radical proposals. This, they say, may become an increasing source of institutional uncertainty. There is also the possibility that voters will overlook the wider consequences of a decision. Take the 2014 vote to restrict immigration of European Union nationals. How many of the yes voters realised that saying No to Mass Immigration (the title of the initiative) would mean jeopardising Switzerland's complex and crucial set of bilateral agreements with its biggest trading partner, the EU? The government has been tying itself in knots since then, faced with the impossible task of meeting the demands of the initiative and keeping an interlinked system of mutual cooperation in place with the EU (see Chapter 11).

Under the current rules, parliament is responsible for checking the contents of proposed initiatives for admissibility. Avenir Suisse says this task should be passed over to the Federal

Chancellery to improve impartiality and avoid conflicts of interest. Most importantly, the research suggests that the signature hurdle is too low at 100,000. It was set at a time when Switzerland's population was half what it is today, and less advanced mobility made the collection of signatures much more onerous. To reflect these changes, the new target should be 210,000 signatures, corresponding to 4% of the electorate. This proposal, among others, was studied and rejected by a Council of States committee that reported in August 2015. The committee was more interested in filters such as applying closer scrutiny to potential initiatives and broadening grounds for declaring them invalid.

Parliament has the task of wording the new laws that stem from initiatives approved by voters. Because this phase is increasingly subject to political wrangling – it goes too far, not far enough, no it doesn't, yes it does – Avenir Suisse recommends that every new piece of legislation based on an initiative should be returned to the electorate for approval. This would avoid the kind of situation that emerged when the Swiss People's Party felt obliged to launch a second deportation initiative in 2012, called the Enforcement Initiative, to ensure that the first initiative was faithfully implemented. Avenir Suisse also wants to see only one measure per voting day. "Voting on multiple proposals on the same day raises the danger of electors having insufficient information on each measure." One subject at a time would probably improve the quality of the debate but it does add up to a lot of voting Sundays.

Annemarie Huber-Hotz is one of the most senior politicians to tackle the overuse of popular initiatives. Huber-Hotz was federal chancellor from 2000 to 2007. She gave a newspaper interview in November 2014 saying that what was now happening departed from the original spirit of the popular initiative. Raising the signatures requirement was not the solution. She proposed a ban on political parties represented in parliament using initiatives to promote their own agenda. "We should rather make sure the popular initiative as a tool remains reserved for those for whom it was originally conceived... The popular initiative was not introduced for the promotion and electioneering of the political parties that are represented in parliament." Not surprisingly, the Council of States committee of serving politicians from those parties did not agree with her.

However, the debate on reform of direct democracy is well and truly launched. Former President Couchepin is on record as saying that direct democracy is not the goal, rather it is a means to an end, and that it can also evolve. In an interview with online news site *watson*, he dismissed the suggestion that such an attitude shook the foundations of Switzerland. "Switzerland was here before direct democracy came along. We have to stop glorifying it, it cannot solve all our problems."

Money and influence

Switzerland is the only member country in the Council of Europe that has not yet introduced legislation on the funding of political parties and general elections. The Council's Group of States Against Corruption (GRECO) noted with regret in its June 2015 report that the Swiss government had decided not to legislate on the issue for the time being. In an earlier evaluation report GRECO made six recommendations to Switzerland on the transparency of political funding, none of which were implemented.

The lack of political will on this issue could not be more obvious. A government delegation met with the party leaders and chairs of parliamentary groups in August 2014, and presented two models for introducing more transparency. "All the parties, apart from the Socialist Party [Social Democrats], came out in favour of maintaining the status quo, with no transparency requirement, since they regard the current system as having proven its usefulness in the case of Switzerland," GRECO reported.

In November 2014, the Swiss government decided not to legislate, on the grounds that the particularities of the Swiss political system were not reconcilable with a law on party funding. The government also argued that it would go against the principles of federalism to impose blanket rules. The national culture of respect for private financial matters also came into play.

"In Switzerland politics and party funding are perceived as a largely private matter, rather than being a state responsibility," the government statement said. The three cantons of Ticino, Geneva and Neuchâtel, each of which has independently introduced transparency requirements in political funding, would disagree.

In Neuchâtel, for example, anonymous donations are prohibited and donors' identities must be disclosed for sums in excess of 5,000 francs. However, political parties are not required to disclose the exact amount paid by each donor, merely the total donations received and a list of donors.

Transparency International Switzerland has repeatedly raised concerns about this issue. It points to the aggravating problem of the possible dependence of a political party on well-resourced interest groups. "We have to admit that political parties are more and more dependent on interest groups, which support parties in connection with specific choices and themes."

The amount of money involved is significant considering the relatively small population. Former secretary general of the Christian Democrats, Hilmar Gernet, has written a book about funding in Swiss politics, *(Un-)heimliches Geld* ([Sinister] Secret Money). He estimates that parties and candidates taking part in the 2015 federal elections spent between 150 million and 170 million francs. The party with by far the strongest spending power is the Swiss People's Party, based on assessments of their advertising spending. A 2011 breakdown produced by *Bilanz* magazine estimated People's Party spending at four times the combined budget of its rivals.

Lobbying is another major part of the political scene. Parliamentary legislative committees play an important role in examining and bringing forward new legislation. Because Swiss parliamentarians are meant to be part-time politicians with jobs in the real world, there is inevitably some cross-pollination between politics and big corporations and other interest groups. It becomes a little worrying when interest groups and large companies appoint parliamentarians to their boards who are members of the very committees that will have an important influence on their field of activity. A *Neue Zürcher Zeitung* survey of the external connections of the newly-elected 2015 members of parliament found that 241 parliamentarians between them represented the interests of 1,671 organisations. The influence comes from across the political spectrum, the paper reported. "Humanitarian and non-profit organisations have more men and women on the ground than farmers. The environment sector is more influential than high finance."

Professional lobbyists are also ever-present in the parliament building. Every elected representative can grant two guest passes to whomever they want, without specifying the nature of that person's business. When parliament is in session, the corridors, café and bar of the Bundeshaus are abuzz with hushed power-broking. Any attempt to scrap the badges-for-mates system and introduce a more transparent accreditation system has fallen on deaf ears in parliament. But there is some unease creeping in about the lack of transparency since a cash-for-question scandal that emerged in May 2015. Radical Party member Christa Markwalder had submitted a parliamentary question in 2013 on relations between Switzerland and Kazakhstan. It turned out that Markwalder had not penned the question herself; it had actually been approved by a Kazakh government official. According to the *Neue Zürcher Zeitung*, a lobbyist working for a public relations firm hired by the Ak-Jol party in Kazakhstan approached Markwalder with the question, offering money for her assistance. This political group, which masquerades as an opposition party, is in fact close to the Kazakh regime. Unknown to Markwalder, the text drafted by the lobbyist had in fact been rewritten by Kazakh government officials. This false step didn't do the 41-year-old politician any lasting harm. *Au contraire.* Spared any sanction by her colleagues, she was re-elected to the National Council in October 2015 and selected shortly afterwards for the prestigious job as speaker of the chamber. Just another reason why the Swiss voters who do bother to vote can be glad they have the final say on anything that comes out of parliament.

Swiss democracy has long attracted admirers. The Russian writer Alexander Solzhenitsyn spent the first two years of his exile in Switzerland, and was highly impressed by the outdoor communal assembly he witnessed in Appenzell Innerrhoden. In a 1974 television interview in the US, he raved about the Swiss system:

> Swiss democracy has some amazing qualities. First, it is completely silent and works inaudibly. Secondly, there is stability. [...] Thirdly, it's an upturned pyramid. That is, there is more power at the local level than in the cantons, and more power in the cantons than with the government. Furthermore, democracy is everyone's responsibility. Each individual would rather moderate their own demands than damage the whole structure. [...] Naturally one can only admire such a democracy.

The Swiss model of true federalism and direct democracy embracing different cultures is often held up as an alternative for established democracies with a tendency to produce hung parliaments, as well as for post-conflict situations. Peter Emerson of the de Borda Institute in Belfast wrote an opinion piece in the *The Irish Times* in April 2016 in which he lamented the fact that Ireland was still without a government 50 days after the general election. He urged the Irish political parties to consider adopting a power-sharing model along the lines of Switzerland (they didn't). At that time, Spain was in the same boat, having reached 100 days post-election without a government. Belgium took the record in 2010–2011 with its political crisis in which the parliament went 20 months without being able to form a government.

Once a year in Fribourg a hopeful gathering takes place of 40 young people from all over the world, at the summer university of the Institute of Federalism. The students, whose fees and costs are paid by the institute with the support of the Swiss Agency for Development and Cooperation, mainly come from countries emerging from conflict or dealing with secessionist movements. Many are citizens of the 34 new states that have joined the world stage since 1990. They learn about federalism, decentralisation and other forms of power sharing. They make connections and discover new ideas. One day, those ideas may even change the world.

CHAPTER 11

The Swiss Are European

It is twenty past six on a breezy Friday morning in the small town of Thonon-les-Bains on the French side of Lake Geneva. I join the early risers hurrying downhill to the jetty on foot, by bicycle and on scooters, on their way to catch a ferry named after a Swiss general. The *Général Guisan* docks and the commuters start to board for the fifty-minute international journey to Lausanne on the northern shore. The French-Swiss border runs through the middle of the lake. Some 600 Thonon residents make this picturesque return trip daily to work outside the European Union. They are among more than 300,000 people who work in Switzerland but live across the border in France, Italy, Germany or Austria, a status known in French as *frontalier*.

Only a handful of people sit in the open air at the bow of the ship, which has capacity for 550 passengers. Most settle at the tables indoors, chatting in small groups or occupied by their own thoughts or phones. The diligent few have their laptops open, work badges already clipped on, and coffee to hand. Others, not yet in work mode, leave their tickets out to be inspected and put their heads down on their arms like tired schoolkids.

"The crossing is a bit long but you can use the time to work if you like," a marketing director tells me, keen to stress that she has not encountered any animosity working in Switzerland.

"I don't see the border as important. We work in the region where we live. It is not complicated to be a *frontalier*."

It is not complicated because, after fifteen years of free movement of labour between Switzerland and the EU, Swiss employers are used to cross-border workers. All the necessary arrangements are in place, including the mutual recognition of professional qualifications, exemption from taxation at source, and coordination of social insurance systems.

Frontaliers now make up 6.3 per cent of the workforce in the canton of Vaud, though that proportion is higher in lower paid jobs. The labour traffic is one way for the simple reason that there is no financial incentive for Swiss residents to work in France. The average gross salary in the Lake Geneva region was 6,558 francs in 2015, compared to 3,538 francs (2,957 euro) next door in 2014 (the franc is stronger now, increasing the gap). The morning boats return to the French side of the lake virtually empty.

By 7.15 a.m. the fifty-minute crossing is almost completed. The passengers with the fold-up scooters are the first to move. They gather near the exit before the boat docks in Lausanne, ready to shoot off to jobs in admin, healthcare, education and industry. With brisk steps, most of the commuters make their way to nearby Ouchy Metro station to catch an early train up the hill to other parts of the city.

Above and beyond anything else, the relationship between Switzerland and the European Union is a human one, with millions of Swiss and EU citizens interacting with each other every day in workplaces, families and communities. Apart from the 318,500 cross-border workers (up from 251,700 in 2011), some 1.4 million EU citizens currently live in Switzerland. Meanwhile 430,000 Swiss citizens live in the EU.

Residents of Thonon-le-Bains begin their morning commute

Closer than close

Many European countries like to say they are located in the heart of Europe; geographically, Switzerland has more claim to that title than most. But politically, Switzerland cannot or will not fit in. At least that's the official position.

In reality, Switzerland is a lot more deeply entwined with the EU than many Swiss people realise. As well as the intensive contact between people – 17.5 per cent of Swiss residents are EU citizens – Switzerland is hooked on the EU because the single market of 510 million people is its largest trading partner. Daily trade between the two amounts to almost a billion Swiss francs. Today, almost 54% of all Switzerland's exports go to the EU and about 72% of its imports come from the EU.

Because of its strategic location on European trade routes, Switzerland has been central to EU road transport policy for decades. The quantity of goods transported over Swiss alpine routes by road and rail reached a total of 39 million tonnes in 2015. Under the EU/Switzerland Land Transport Agreement, Switzerland liberalised its rail transport market and scrapped its own weight limits for heavy goods vehicles in favour of EU limits.

Although it is not part of the EU customs union, Switzerland has open borders with the 26-country Schengen area, which means no systematic passport controls on travellers. From 2007 to 2017 it paid one billion francs into the EU cohesion funds, supporting energy efficiency, public transport, microcredit and traffic calming projects, for example, in the new EU states. In addition, every piece of new Swiss legislation is checked for its euro-compatibility so that large swathes of national legislation are effectively copy-pasted from Brussels.

Switzerland's dealings with the EU are governed by a web of more than 20 main bilateral agreements and around 100 other agreements. Known as the Bilateral Agreements I and II, they were negotiated in two bundles between 1994 and 1999, and 2002 and 2004 respectively.

The first group covered research, air and road transportation, public procurement, the free movement of persons, and technical barriers to trade and agriculture. The second covered agricultural products, statistics, pensions, environment, media, the fight against fraud, taxation of savings and the Schengen/Dublin accords relating to internal security.

As explained by the Swiss Mission to the European Union in Brussels, "On the one hand, these agreements create wide-ranging mutual access to markets; on the other, they provide the basis for close cooperation in important policy areas such as research, security, environment and culture. The agreements governing market access are as a rule based on existing EU law in which Switzerland has undertaken to enact equivalent provisions or to adopt existing EU law."

These bilateral agreements are currently managed through a structure of more than 15 joint committees. The Swiss ostensibly have their freedom but without a voice to influence the policy they end up following.

Swiss-EU ties are increasing rather than diminishing. To name just three examples: a bilateral agreement creating mutual free access in the electricity market is in the works; the two partners are also working on linking up their emissions trading systems for CO_2 emissions allowances; Switzerland and the EU also want to become better integrated in the areas of food safety and public health, for example by Swiss participation in the European Food Safety Authority, an EU agency. Switzerland is also a member of the EU's Horizon 2020, a seven-year 80-billion-euro research and innovation programme.

A bridge too far
If Switzerland is so close to the EU that it could almost pass for a member, what is stopping the country from joining the club? Scepticism and self-determination. The Swiss cannot overlook the fact that the EU is a supranational organisation that requires member states to cede some of their decision-making powers to community institutions. Such a move would be unthinkable to the alpine nation because it is deemed incompatible with the Swiss political system of direct democracy. The EU is widely criticised for its perceived democratic deficit.

There are economic arguments too. The current system is complicated, but it works, as the trade figures show. Switzerland makes hay with the EU and remains free to negotiate trade agreements with third countries. Switzerland's successful 2013 free trade agreement with China is a good example. The EU currently has no such agreement in place with the economic giant of Asia.

The argument hardly needs to be made because no one is suggesting membership as a viable course of action. That would be political suicide. The pro-EU membership camp in Switzerland has been beaten down over the years, barely raising its voice above a whisper these days. A gfs.bern poll conducted in February 2017 put public support for membership at just 15 per cent. The predominant Swiss view is that the EU project is rather unwieldy and misguided, while hardliners go much further, painting the EU as a hostile entity completely without merit.

The Swiss People's Party strongman, Christoph Blocher, has been leading the charge against the EU for decades. Blocher does not so much call a spade a spade as call it a dangerous implement of foreign interference. In his analysis, the EU is the opposite of all the good things Switzerland stands for. The EU is the enemy, motivated by "envy, ill will and greed", and those Swiss who seek closer ties are collaborators. This description from a speech at his party's conference in Biel in June 2017 makes his position clear.

> Undemocratic, centralist, run by functionaries and centralist-minded politicians, hardly any of them democratically elected. Switzerland grew organically; the EU is an intellectual construct! More precisely: a failed intellectual construct....

> This [Switzerland's] successful way must not be sacrificed, neither by doubting, nor by self-serving politicians, nor by traitorous functionaries, nor by managers who are unable to see past the ends of their noses, apart from looking into their own wallets.

The EU has had a rough few years since the eurozone crisis began in 2009, unable to break out of the negative news cycle that culminated in the shock of the United Kingdom's vote in June 2016 to leave the union.

But this slap in the face has had an unexpected effect. Far from sparking a rush to the exit by other countries, the Brexit decision has actually boosted Europeans' loyalty to the EU. Approval ratings for the union have surged, up 18 percentage points in both Germany and France a year after Brexit. In the same survey from the Pew Research Center, even UK residents had a more positive view of the EU (54 per cent approval, up 10 percentage points from the previous year). A median of just 18 per cent in the nine continental EU nations surveyed wanted their own country to leave the EU.

The EU also has an important role to play on the world stage. The arrival of a new US President with his hostile 'America First' posturing and weak stance on Russia has also highlighted the importance of a strong EU to protect Europe's interests.

Dangerous gamble

15 February 2014 was a depressing day for EU citizens living in Switzerland, including myself. It was the day that Swiss voters, by the slimmest of majorities (50.3 per cent), sent a message to us that we were unwelcome. The disappointment I felt was akin to discovering that a friend believed malicious rumours about me, despite the many years of mutual support and good times we shared.

Emotions aside, the vote to restrict the free movement of EU citizens after twelve years of unrestricted two-way migration put the Swiss government in a devilishly difficult position. It also showed that Swiss direct democracy in matters affecting the EU has its limits, even if the country is a non-member.

When negotiations on the first set of Bilateral Agreements between the EU and Switzerland got bogged down by political developments in Switzerland in the 1990s, the EU insisted that the seven main treaties within Bilateral Agreements I had to be linked by a "guillotine clause". If one treaty is breached, they all collapse. The free movement of persons was one of the seven. This condition raised the stakes after the 2014 immigration quotas vote. If the government did implement the will of the people, they would jeopardise a crucial deal that ensured prosperity and stability for the country. Many nervous months followed in which the EU froze all negotiations and the Swiss tried to come up with a palatable solution within a three-year deadline.

A proposed way out of the dead-end was passed by parliament in December 2016. Variously described as a U-turn, a climbdown and a pirouette, the compromise avoids imposing quotas, taking the lesser step of forcing employers to give Swiss residents priority when filling new job vacancies. Family firms are exempt and the priority rules only apply to sectors or regions with above-average unemployment.

Despite huffing and puffing from the advocates of the initiative about capitulation and treason, it was understood by the public (58 per cent in a March 2017 poll) and parliament that the EU agreements were more important than implementing to the letter the constitutional changes set out in the immigration vote.

It has now been demonstrated that the Swiss are not foolhardy enough to defend the principle of direct democracy at any price. The lesson has also been learned that at least one of the four core EU freedoms – the free movement of persons – is effectively untouchable if you are a smaller negotiating partner in Europe. United Kingdom take note.

It's complicated

In the lead-up to the Brexit vote, the Swiss case was held up as a successful alternative to EU membership, one the British could potentially emulate. But since the leave vote of June 2016, and the closer inspection of the ramifications of that decision that followed, the realisation has dawned that the complex Swiss model is not an arrangement any other country could replicate, however they might wish to replicate Swiss economic success.

Why not? The truth is there are drawbacks to the current arrangements on both sides and a new model is actively being sought. On one side of the table, the EU has had enough of negotiating dozens of tailor-made deals for the Swiss and of having to constantly oversee updates. While the bilateral treaties are static, EU law is not. Therefore, the larger partner now wants a streamlined arrangement with Switzerland that rolls all the agreements into one framework with a built-in update function. For example, when the EU changes its regulations on information included in drug packaging, the laws in member states automatically follow suit. The EU wants such automatic updates to happen in Switzerland too. The new model is going by the not-so-catchy title of "institutional framework agreement".

The new agreement is quite a difficult concept to explain to Swiss voters, who will ultimately have to approve it in the likely event of a referendum. Blocher has already founded the "committee against creeping EU membership" to fight the agreement before it comes into being. Yet the institutional framework is make-or-break for the EU. The Council of the EU has repeatedly stressed that such a framework is required to continue mutual access for the EU and Switzerland to the markets in the sectors governed by the bilateral agreements. Negotiations started in May 2014 and are behind schedule. One of the main sticking points is what procedures should be used to settle disputes between Switzerland and the EU. This raises the spectre of foreign courts telling the Swiss what to do, sacrilege in the eyes of the People's Party, which has another popular initiative coming up entitled: "Swiss law instead of foreign judges (initiative for self-determination)".

On the Swiss side of the table, negotiators are subject to the whims of the Swiss public, who have been convinced that the so-called bilateral way in its current incarnation is a win-win for Switzerland. They see this special treatment as a point of pride, and anything that smacks of more integration into the EU will be a hard sell.

Switzerland and the EU are like the long-term couple who are not married but have cobbled together most of the equivalent rights and obligations. They have been to a lawyer to arrange a bunch of contracts covering next of kin, parental rights, wills, property and pensions, and they enjoy all the joys and tribulations of matrimony. But scratch the surface and you will find that one of the parties is not happy and is pushing for more commitment.

In theory, another option would be for Switzerland to slot into an existing group of non-EU members in Europe with a ready-made list of terms and conditions, a civil partnership of sorts. The European Economic Area (EEA) was created specifically for this purpose but Swiss voters rejected joining the EEA in a 1992 vote that still has repercussions today.

This is a good juncture to look at the past and see what brought about the Swiss exception in the first place.

Alphabet soup
In the post-war period, the countries of Western Europe were keen to create alliances to foster economic development and

WHEN SWITZERLAND JOINED
INTERNATIONAL ORGANISATIONS / AGREEMENTS

1948*
OECD
(then OEEC)

1960*
EFTA

1963
Council of Europe

1972
Free Trade
Agreement EEC

1973
OSCE

1992
World Bank

1992
IMF

1992
EEA NO

1996
NATO's
Partnership for Peace

2002
UN

2008
Schengen

*Founding member

promote peace. Switzerland was on board for the first of these alliances – now known as the Organisation for Economic Co-operation and Development (OECD) – launched in 1948 by 20 founding countries.

Then came the forerunner to today's European Union, the European Economic Community (EEC), which was established in 1957 by the Treaties of Rome, and included only six countries: West Germany, Italy, France, Belgium, The Netherlands and Luxembourg.

The next development in European alliances was the founding of the European Free Trade Association (EFTA) in Stockholm three years later in 1960. As a counterbalance to the EEC, Switzerland together with six other European countries established EFTA, scrapping customs duties on trade amongst its members.

Six versus seven. That sounds fair. And things could have motored along nicely like that if it wasn't for the problem of defections. At first the EFTA team was up two members, when Finland (1961, associate member) and Iceland (1970, full member) joined. Meanwhile other members of EFTA were planning their exit, virtually from day one. The UK and Denmark finally bid adieu and joined the EEC in 1973. Portugal followed in 1985.

Switzerland was not a special case vis-à-vis the EU during these years, concluding a Free Trade Agreement with the EEC Nine in 1972, the same agreement used by the other EFTA countries (with different annexes). This agreement formed the basis of future Swiss-EU bilateral agreements.

Drama of 1992

Relations between Switzerland and EU are still defined by developments that took place in 1992, which is why we now need to spend some time in the era of fax machines and plaid flannel shirts.

First, the global context: The Soviet Union was dissolved on 26 December 1991, leaving Boris Yeltsin as president of the newly independent Russian Federation. Bill Clinton was campaigning for president, an election he won in November. The Maastricht Treaty was signed in February, which founded the twelve-member European Union. War broke out in newly independent Bosnia and Herzegovina in April. The uptake of email was still in the future and "Rhythm is a Dancer" by Snap! was European number one for thirteen consecutive weeks.

Throughout the 1960s, 1970s and 1980s, the Swiss government had maintained its scepticism towards the EEC. As a supranational organ, with policy planned and controlled by a group of nations, this union was not thought to be compatible with the Swiss system of direct democracy. Swiss sovereignty was at stake.

The playing field changed at the end of the 1980s, when Jacques Delors, then president of the European Commission, offered EFTA states a form of partnership called the European Economic Area. This would give EFTA states the advantages of EU integration without ceding any sovereignty – and without participation in the EU decision-making processes.

The offer was attractive for the Swiss government as an alternative to EU membership, and the project of the EEA treaty was passed by parliament easily. All that remained was to get the approval of voters, and a referendum date was set for 6 December 1992.

Most EFTA countries viewed the EEA as a provisional arrangement, a sort of halfway house on the road to full EU membership. This became clear when Austria, Sweden, Finland and Norway asked the EU to initiate accession negotiations.

Over three decades, the Swiss integration strategy with the EU and its forerunners had broadly been determined by observing what Switzerland's "allied partners" in EFTA, fellow neutrals Austria and Sweden, did, according to political scientist Thomas Gees.

"For Switzerland – as well as for other EFTA countries – the years between 1989 and 1992 marked a period of change in the history of European integration. Historians in Switzerland agree that the [Swiss] government fundamentally changed its approach to the European integration process," Gees writes in his essay on the transnational perspective of the Swiss government's application to join the EC (see bibliography).

Within this four-year period, which also saw the reunification of Germany and the collapse of the Soviet Union, the Federal Council published three reports to explain its strategy to parliament and the public. The option to join the EC/EU was initially ranked third, but after negotiations on the EEA in 1992 it was the preferred option.

Not wanting to be left behind in a rapidly-changing European constellation, the Swiss government lodged its own application with Brussels within weeks of signing the EEA treaty in May 1992.

This move has variously been described by specialists as a "stupendous acceleration" (Laurent Goetschel) and "a rupture with the past" (Pascal Sciarini).

Overnight, the EEA vote became an EU vote and the debate was blown wide open. This was the moment Christoph Blocher really became a household name, when he criss-crossed the country holding rallies against EEA membership. If voters had been jittery about the EEA, they were downright alarmed by the last-minute moving of the goalposts. In the end, the proposal to join the EEA was rejected in December 1992 by 50.3% of voters as well as 18 of the 26 cantons.

Opponents of Switzerland joining the EEA highlighted the threats to the traditional political culture. "In a long and emotional campaign, they mobilized against the loss of national sovereignty and neutrality, against loss of political self-determination and against foreign jurisdiction implied by the treaty," Swiss political scientist Wolf Linder explains in his essay, "Europe and Switzerland, Europeanization without EU membership".

There would be no EU membership, not even a stepping stone towards membership. The application was "frozen" by the Swiss in 1993 and remained on ice until it was withdrawn in 2016.

The vote exposed the deep political divide between the more pro-European French-speakers (80% voted yes) and the more isolationist German-speakers (62% voted no), leaving the former group with a bitter taste and a sense of powerlessness for years to come. The day after the vote the French language *La Liberté* newspaper ran the front-page headline "The French-speaking Swiss reject the ghetto constructed by the German speakers."

The voters' rejection of the EEA showed the strength of direct democracy, which could wipe out years of work by the political administration in a single stroke. The Swiss government bounced back a few months later by presenting the EU with a list of 15 proposed topics for bilateral negotiation. The bilateral way was born.

Conclusion

The EU rejected by the Swiss in 1992 has changed beyond recognition. Some argue the expansion of the bloc to include Eastern European countries was too much, too soon and has had a destabilising effect. But we cannot compare this historic choice with alternatives that never happened. Citizens of the "new" EU states are naturally glad of the benefits inclusion has brought. Yet, the introduction of a single currency to a group

of countries with completely different economic profiles is another of the EU's weak points, as painfully demonstrated by the eurozone debt crisis. Most recently, the EU's lack of unity in dealing with the refugee crisis has exposed an absence of common values. On top of all this comes the fear and division sown by frequent terrorist attacks, and the shock of Brexit in 2016.

In December 2016, John Cassidy wrote in *The New Yorker* that Europe was a continent sorely lacking in hope and optimism. "Although the majority of Europeans still support the EU, and appreciate the peace and relative harmony that it has helped to preserve for sixty years, the passion and sense of being on the right side of history have ebbed."

Observing these troubles from their shipshape country, the Swiss can be forgiven for feeling glad to be out of the mess. But it cannot be denied that Switzerland is richer, smarter and more productive thanks to the EU. The ready availability of cross-border workers and EU citizens coming to live in Switzerland has boosted Swiss economic growth over the past 15 years, according to a large body of research. One 2017 report by the Swiss Secretariat for Economic Affairs concluded that free movement had increased the number of high-skilled jobs in the country and reoriented the Swiss economy towards high-value activity. Close cooperation with the EU on research, security and the environment has also brought significant benefits. The Swiss health, agriculture and tourist sectors would grind to a halt without EU labour.

But that doesn't mean that everyone is happy, and the isolationist tune is still popular. In his writings, interviews and speeches about Europe, Blocher lambastes the "arrogant Bern elite", who place no value on Switzerland's special case status, and are busily "sawing away the branch upon which Switzerland sits". Meanwhile, the majority of the country's elected representatives and the career civil servants who carry out their directives work within the reality that no arrangement with the EU can be crafted that will not in some way impinge on Switzerland's delicate sovereignty. The fear is that the vocal anti-Europe movement will spook the electorate and undo more years of work, endangering EU relations and consequently the Swiss economy.

Blocher's long-time rival, former president Pascal Couchepin, has pleaded for more respect towards the EU. In a 2014 interview with *Watson News* he gave the following warning: "If we want to find a way out of this difficult situation, we have to stop degrading the EU. Particularly in German-speaking Switzerland I feel an unbelievable antipathy, or even hatred towards the EU. Why? The EU has achieved a lot and is a chance for the world."

The most honest and pragmatic solution for Switzerland now would probably be to apply to join the European Economic Area on the same terms as fellow EFTA countries Norway, Iceland and Liechtenstein, and save teams of negotiators years of work cobbling together a close imitation. But honest solutions are not always possible in politics. The EU taboo is so strong in Switzerland that even the EEA is a contaminated brand. No political party is yet willing to touch it. And so the merry dance continues. Until relations with the EU are reorganised on a more satisfactory and sustainable footing, this unresolved issue will remain a thorn in the side of Switzerland, eating up time and energy that could be expended on other pressing national questions.

It may be premature to say, but, in the return of some economic stability, election results based more on hope than fear, and renewed unity after Brexit, there are signs that the EU might be turning a corner. Voices predicting its imminent demise have fallen silent, for now. As Europeans, the Swiss have no choice but to wish the EU well.

For such a small country, Switzerland and its people have accumulated a plethora of clichés. The heart-warming image of Heidi running into Grandfather's arms in an alpine meadow vies with the darker one of soulless bankers filling the vaults of Zurich with ill-gotten gains. In between these iconic extremes, ordinary Swiss people live the Swiss reality unnoticed and a little unloved. This book has attempted to portray that reality and the Swiss character, in good faith.

I did not set out to heap starry-eyed praise on the Swiss; neither did I want to indulge in self-righteous condemnation. In writing this book, I was driven by a desire to get the facts straight, and for those facts to be fair and accurate. But the facts are not enough. To really understand a nation, you have to get to know its people, and I hope I've done my bit with the introductions here.

I love the Dostoyevsky quotes about Switzerland. I recognise that impotent anger because I felt it once myself. You get the sense that this man was stuck in an environment that did not suit or please him, and he was lashing out. But with the Swiss, as with any nationality whose space you are sharing as an immigrant or visitor, you have to move eventually beyond the Dostoyevsky phase of hypercritical judgment. A superhuman effort is required to progress from being a linguistic, cultural and social outsider to carving out a place for yourself in a new society. Three cheers for anyone who has managed it.

An early working title of this book was *A Doomed Attempt to Undo the Curse of the Cuckoo Clock*. I don't think I need to remind English speakers about the famous Harry Lime quote from the *The Third Man* about the cuckoo clock being all the

Swiss had to show for 500 years of brotherly love and democracy. If nothing else, I hope in these pages to have introduced you to enough compelling individuals and features of Swissness to banish the idea that the Swiss can be dismissed with a condescending one-liner.

Over the past century, Europe has followed two strong trends, neither of which the Swiss adopted. The first was the trend of slaughter on an apocalyptic scale; the second, the trend of political unity. We may, post-Brexit, be seeing the beginning of a third trend now. Assuming the role of resolute outsiders in the European community of nations has created an "us-and-them" rift. When the Swiss refuse to hitch their wagon to the common destiny of Europe, it does come across as a little superior. True enough, there is a supremacist streak being expressed in the Swiss political spectrum today, and it is the least attractive side of modern Switzerland. But stronger than this streak is the national desire to do the right thing, which gives me hope for the future. One thing I would like see Switzerland do now, especially in the light of its historic failure towards persecuted Jews during the Second World War, would be to provide shelter more proactively to today's desperate refugees, and not keep our heads down, hoping the routes of the dispossessed will pass us by. Another thing that is crying out for a change of approach is the country's naturalisation policy. All the tough talk at political levels translates on the ground into an arbitrary, discriminatory and disheartening system for future citizens. Finally, I hope the Swiss will continue to use their privileged position to seek better models for the fair organisation of society and the protection of the environment.

I've asked a lot of questions in this book. Each chapter has taken an assumption about the Swiss and attempted to test the ratio between truth and prejudice behind it. If Swiss readers have also enjoyed seeing their culture from a different perspective, and maybe even begun to reflect on familiar facts differently, I will consider this time well spent. I don't want to make up your minds for you, I want you to feel well-enough informed to come to your own conclusions about the naked Swiss.

Whether you are at the stage of being puzzled, frustrated or charmed by Switzerland, I hope this read has been an interesting part of the journey.

Clare O'Dea, December 2017
Fribourg, Switzerland
clareodea.com

The **Federal Council** (*Bundesrat, Conseil Fédéral*), elected by the **Federal Assembly** (both chambers of parliament together), is the highest executive authority in the country, the equivalent of a cabinet, with seven members representing the four largest political parties, each of whom heads a government department. Decisions are made by consensus. Also referred to in English as the government or the cabinet.

The Swiss parliament has two chambers. The **National Council** (*Nationalrat* or *Conseil National*), also known as the House of Representatives in English, has 200 members and is elected every four years according to a system of proportional election. Each of the 26 cantons has a number of seats that corresponds to population size.

The **Council of States** (*Ständerat* or *Conseil des États*), also known as the Senate in English, has 46 members, returned by the cantons. Each canton has two seats in the Council of States, with the exception of the six so-called half cantons (formerly larger cantons that split in two at different points in history) – Basel-Landschaft, Basel City, Appenzell Innerrhoden, Appenzell Ausserrhoden, Obwalden and Nidwalden – which each have one seat. The Federal Assembly normally convenes in Bern four times a year for three-week sittings.

The **Swiss People's Party** (*Schweizer Volkspartei*, SVP, *Union Démocratique du Centre*, UDC), Switzerland's biggest and best-funded party with almost 30% of the popular vote, has a conservative-right nationalist platform. Traditionally drew support from farmers and the small business community but has broadened its base. Pro-army, anti-immigration, for stricter asylum policy and more security. Professes to defend real Swiss values and way of life.

The **Social Democrats** (SP, *Sozial-Demokratische Partei* or PS, *Parti Socialiste*) are the traditional opposition to right-leaning Swiss politics. With 18% of the vote in the last general elections, the Social Democrats have lost ground in recent years. Left-wing, the party believes in strong public services and a good welfare net, social equality and protection of the environment. "An economy for the people and not the other way round."

FDP The Liberals (FDP stands for *Freisinnig-Demokratische Partei* or Liberal Democratic Party, *Parti Libéral Radical* in French) have been continually in government since the foundation of the state. Popular with the self-employed and the professions, the centre-right party merged with the smaller Liberal Party of Switzerland in 2009 and now goes by the name FDP The Liberals. Also known as the Radicals in English. With a pro-business ethos, the party identifies its core values as freedom, public spirit and progress.

The **Christian Democrats** (*Christlichdemokratische Volkspartei der Schweiz*, CVP, *Parti Démocrate-Chrétien*, PDC) were originally a conservative Catholic-based party popular in rural areas. The party still supports family values ("people and the community in the centre") but has moved to a more centrist position, closer on some social issues to the Social Democrats. Rejects "simplified ideology", wanting Switzerland to be economically strong as well as a caring society.

Apart from the big four, a further eight political parties are represented in parliament, including the Green Party and the Green Liberals.

Begert, Roland, Lange Jahre Fremd (Edition Liebefeld, 2008)

Bewes, Diccon, *Swiss Watching, Inside the Land of Milk & Money*, (Nicholas Brealey Publishing, 2010)

Bornstein, Heini, *Insel Schweiz* (Chronos Verlag, 2000)

Breiding, R. James, *Swiss Made* (Profile Books, 2013)

Church, Clive H. (edited by), *Switzerland and the European Union, A close contradictory and misunderstood relationship* (Routledge Taylor & Francis Group 2007)

Codevilla, Angelo M., *Between the Alps and a Hard Place, Switzerland in World War II and the Rewriting of History* (Regnery Publishing, 2000)

Einstein, Albert, Erinnerungen (p. 145–153), Schweizerische Hochshulzeitung (periodical), Volume 28 (Leemann, 1955)

Fischer, Thomas & Gehler, Michael (edited by), *Next Door. Aspects in comparison of Switzerland, Liechtenstein, Austria and Germany*, (Böhlau Verlag, 2014)

Fraser, Antonia, *Marie Antoinette The Journey* (Phoenix 2002)

Haver, Gianni, Mix & Remix, *Swissness in a Nutshell* (Bergli Books 2014)

Meyer, Helmut & Schneebeli, Peter, *Durch Geschichte zur Gegenwart 3* (Lehrmittelvertrag Zurich)

Koydl, Wolfgang, *Wer hat's erfunden? Unter Schweizern*, (Ullstein Buchverlage, 2012)

Kreis, Georg, *Switzerland in the Second World War, Responding to the Challenges of the Time* (Pro Helvetia, 1999)

Edited by Kreis, Georg, *Switzerland and the Second World War* (Frank Cass, 2000)

Edited by Muirhead, Russel L., *The Blue Guides, Switzerland* (Ernest Benn Limited London, 1948)

New, Mitya, *Switzerland Unwrapped, Exposing the Myths* (I. B. Tauris, 1997)

Oertig Davidson, Margaret, *Beyond Chocolate*, (Bergli Books, 2011)

Rogger, Franziska, *"Gebt den Schweizerinnen ihre Geschichte!» Marthe Gosteli, ihr Archiv und der übersehene Kampf ums Frauenstimmrecht* (Neue Zürcher Zeitung Verlag, 2014)

Rooney, Padraig, *The Gilded Chalet: Off-piste in Literary Switzerland* (Nicholas Brealey Publishing, 2015)

Sarasin, Philipp, Wecker, Regina, *Raubgold Reduit Flüchtlinge* (Chronos, 1998)

Simonet, Michel, *Une rose et un balai* (Faim de siècle, 2015)

Trampusch, Christine & Mach, André (edited by), *Switzerland in Europe Continuity and change in the Swiss political economy* (Routledge Taylor & Francis Group 2011)

Vogler, Robert U., *Swiss Banking Secrecy: Origins, Significance, Myth* (Association for Financial History, 2006)

Windisch, Uli, *La Suisse, clichés, délire, réalité* (Editions L'Age d'Homme, Lausanne, 1998)

Edited by Wylie, Neville, *European Neutrals and Non-Belligerents during the Second World War* (Cambridge University Press, 2002)

Wylie, Neville, *Britain, Switzerland and the Second World War* (Oxford University Press, 2003)

Chapter 1
House of Switzerland, courtesy of Presence Switzerland
Honegger poster, courtesy of Honegger AG
Winterreise über den Gotthard (Winter journey over the Gotthard), collection Stich von Rothe from a drawing by Jentzsch. Source: Wikimedia Commons.

Chapter 2
Minimum wage initiative, Keystone, Salvatore di Nolfi

Chapter 4
Solar Impulse, copyright Solar Impulse | Ackermann | Rezo
House of Bethlehem
Victorinox, courtesy of Victorinox. Copyright (Photopress/Victorinox)

Chapter 5
Women's vote: Mouvement démocrate chrétien, [1940–1953] DA 1565 Bibliothèque de Genève
Marthe Gosteli at the Gosteli Archive, Clare O'Dea
Mothers in employment, data courtesy of the Federal Statistics Office
Marijka Moser in Solothurn, Clare O'Dea

Chapter 6
Registration of Cuban refugees, copyright Luc Chessex, Lausanne.
Swissint: change of command from the SWISSCOY contingent 33 to contingent 34 at the airport in Pristina/Kosovo,

courtesy of SWISSINT or Swiss Armed Forces International Command.
Bullet production line, Keystone, Alessandro della Valle

Chapter 7
Local defence: Schweizerisches Bundesarchiv
    E5792#1988/204#633*, Ortswehr Verteidigung, 1940.
Military internees: Stadelmann Private achive
Eduard von Steiger, Keystone, STR

Chapter 8
Hiking trail, Clare O'Dea
Michel Simonet, courtesy of faim de siècle publishers, copyright
    Charly Rappo

Chapter 9
Banking cheese cartoon, copyright Chappatte
Banker with purse mouth, copyright Chappatte

Chapter 10
Bundesplatz, Keystone, Peter Klaunzer
Political brochures, Clare O'Dea

Chapter 11
Thonon-les-Bains, Clare O'Dea; EU Crise, Copyright Chappatte.

ACKNOWLEDGEMENTS

I would like to thank some individuals who were generous with their time and expertise during the researching and writing of this book, including the late Marthe Gosteli and Monika Bill of the Gosteli Foundation, Irving Dunn, Marijka Moser, Patricia Widmer, Georg Kreis, Luc Chessex, Neville Wylie, Peter Collmer, Jakob Ackermann, Maria von Känel, Roland Begert, Teodoro and Maddalena Potenza, Claude Baumann, Thomas Gees and Pascal Couchepin.

A special thanks to my former colleagues from SWI *swissinfo. ch*, particularly Urs Geiser and Matthew Allen for their input. Many thanks also to the English Department editors who encouraged me to work on the stories that interested me and helped improve my knowledge of Switzerland – Dale Bechtel, Federico Bragagnini and Christophe Giovannini. My years at swissinfo.ch provided me with an opportunity to accumulate insights into many of the issues covered in this book.

I am particularly indebted to Richard Harvell of Bergli Books for his excellent guidance and editing expertise, and for making this book possible.

Merci vielmal to Jeannette Schär Dias and my parents-in-law Ruth and Paul Zbinden for their generous help with lunches and childcare. Thanks also to the extended Zbinden family. I benefitted greatly from having access to the fantastic resources and working space of the Fribourg Cantonal Library, which could chase up any book in Switzerland within 24 hours. Thanks also to Patrick Furter for the books.

Míle buíochas to my Irish family, particularly my mother Máire O'Dea, Helen O'Dea and Ruth O'Dea. I am also grateful to Karen O'Sullivan for her support and last-minute inspiration and to Kim Hays and Jessica Dacey for their invaluable assistance.

This book is dedicated to the person who first introduced me to Switzerland, my husband, Thomas Zbinden, who has shown unending patience and great support throughout my writing journey. And finally, a big thank you to my wonderful Swiss-Irish girls – Maeve, Ciara and Ashley.

INDEX